REMOTELY POSSIBLE

STRATEGIC LESSONS AND TACTICAL BEST PRACTICES FOR REMOTE WORK

Shawn Belling

Apress®

Remotely Possible: Strategic Lessons and Tactical Best Practices for Remote Work

Shawn Belling
Fitchburg, WI, USA

ISBN-13 (pbk): 978-1-4842-7007-3   ISBN-13 (electronic): 978-1-4842-7008-0
https://doi.org/10.1007/978-1-4842-7008-0

Copyright © 2021 by Shawn Belling

This work is subject to copyright. All rights are reserved by the Publisher, whether the whole or part of the material is concerned, specifically the rights of translation, reprinting, reuse of illustrations, recitation, broadcasting, reproduction on microfilms or in any other physical way, and transmission or information storage and retrieval, electronic adaptation, computer software, or by similar or dissimilar methodology now known or hereafter developed.

Trademarked names, logos, and images may appear in this book. Rather than use a trademark symbol with every occurrence of a trademarked name, logo, or image we use the names, logos, and images only in an editorial fashion and to the benefit of the trademark owner, with no intention of infringement of the trademark.

The use in this publication of trade names, trademarks, service marks, and similar terms, even if they are not identified as such, is not to be taken as an expression of opinion as to whether or not they are subject to proprietary rights.

While the advice and information in this book are believed to be true and accurate at the date of publication, neither the authors nor the editors nor the publisher can accept any legal responsibility for any errors or omissions that may be made. The publisher makes no warranty, express or implied, with respect to the material contained herein.

    Managing Director, Apress Media LLC: Welmoed Spahr
    Acquisitions Editor: Shiva Ramachandran
    Development Editor: Matthew Moodie
    Coordinating Editor: Nancy Chen, Rita Fernando

Cover designed by eStudioCalamar

Distributed to the book trade worldwide by Springer Science+Business Media New York, 1 New York Plaza, New York, NY 100043. Phone 1-800-SPRINGER, fax (201) 348-4505, e-mail orders-ny@springer-sbm.com, or visit www.springeronline.com. Apress Media, LLC is a California LLC and the sole member (owner) is Springer Science + Business Media Finance Inc (SSBM Finance Inc). SSBM Finance Inc is a **Delaware** corporation.

For information on translations, please e-mail booktranslations@springernature.com; for reprint, paperback, or audio rights, please e-mail bookpermissions@springernature.com.

Apress titles may be purchased in bulk for academic, corporate, or promotional use. eBook versions and licenses are also available for most titles. For more information, reference our Print and eBook Bulk Sales web page at http://www.apress.com/bulk-sales.

Any source code or other supplementary material referenced by the author in this book is available to readers on GitHub via the book's product page, located at www.apress.com/978-1-4842-7007-3. For more detailed information, please visit http://www.apress.com/source-code.

Printed on acid-free paper

This book is dedicated to my wife, Jody. Thank you for your loving support and encouragement and for feeding me at my desk during writing and editing sessions.

This book is also dedicated to colleagues past and present with whom I have had the pleasure and privilege of working and learning remotely.

Contents

About the Author vii
Acknowledgments ix
Introduction xi

Chapter 1:   Lessons from a Pandemic 1
Chapter 2:   Things We Knew 13
Chapter 3:   What Will Change 27
Chapter 4:   Leading Virtual/ Remote Teams and Organizations 41
Chapter 5:   Psychology of Remote Teams 59
Chapter 6:   Practices and Tools 75
Chapter 7:   Remotely Successful 91
Chapter 8:   Remote Arguments 101
Chapter 9:   Epilogue 115

Bibliography 123
Index 129

About the Author

Shawn Belling is a globally experienced technology executive and project management speaker and instructor. In a career spanning 30 years, he has held executive and leadership roles in higher education, software, consulting, bio-pharma, manufacturing, and regulatory compliance, and is currently the Chief Information Officer at a large regional technical college. He has over 15 years of experience leading or as part of remote teams and organizations and over a decade of experience teaching graduate-level courses on virtual and remote project team leadership.

As a member of the Project Management Institute, he has spoken regularly at conferences and seminars since 2008, including multiple presentations at PMI Global Conferences in the United States and APAC.

Shawn teaches at the University of Wisconsin–Madison in Engineering Professional Development and the Center for Professional and Executive Development, at the University of Wisconsin–Platteville in the Master of Science – Project Management program, and at the University of Southern California in the Master of Science – Project Management program.

Shawn earned bachelor's and master's degrees from University of Wisconsin schools and is completing a doctorate at the University of the Cumberlands. Shawn is certified by PMI as a Project Management Professional and Agile Certified Practitioner, is a Certified Scrum Professional and Certified Scrum@Scale Practitioner, and is certified in Organizational Change Leadership from the University of Wisconsin–Platteville.

Acknowledgments

I acknowledge the contributions of EDL Consulting and CloudCraze founder Bill Loumpouridis. I interviewed Bill for this book, and while I worked with him, his examples of company culture and working practices taught me what a successful remote distributed organization looks like. Bill also supported me in my career and provided me and others at EDL and CloudCraze with some of our careers' most exciting and rewarding opportunities.

I also acknowledge the late Dr. Ginger Levin. As a professor and mentor, Dr. Levin encouraged me to pursue teaching, writing, and a doctorate. Dr. Levin's course in leading remote teams was my first exposure to the formal techniques associated with remote work, and it is with respect and humility that I now teach and periodically revise the course that she created.

Introduction

If you are reading this, the odds are high that you spent most of 2020 and 2021 in a working environment that was quite different from what you were used to. If you had to pivot to a remote work scenario that was completely new to you, you perhaps found this jarring, empowering, interesting, or confusing. If you are a leader trying to figure out what the future of work holds now that everyone knows remote, distributed work models are a viable option, this book is for you.

I was fortunate. I had opportunities to work and lead remotely from 2005 to 2017 and even taught graduate courses that dealt with aspects of globally distributed remote teams and collaborations. When the Covid-19 pandemic emerged, I spoke to other organizations and leaders trying to navigate this scenario for the first time and offered what advice and assistance I could. I also had the idea of writing a book that would speak to leaders and organizations seeking to learn from the experience and perhaps permanently implement a remote model.

In this book, I draw upon my experiences working in various remote situations as a team member, a leader, and a professor. I have seen good and bad implementations of remote work, and I know what "good" looks like. I also draw upon examples of several organizations that have been highly successful with remote distributed work models as a core part of their overall operating model. I use examples from the many contemporary instances and lived experiences of companies and prominent people during the 2020–2021 timeframe during which a global remote work experiment took place.

I speak to specific practices, culture, and leadership and their place in enabling successful remote work. At the center of this book and all the thinking and guidance in it, the concept of work as something one does versus someplace one goes is critical. I recognize that not every profession or work scenario lends itself to remote or distributed situations – let's get that out of the way. My hope and intent are to offer you practical ideas on implementing remote and distributed work options because you have had the experience yourself and now know that you will do well to make it a part of your organizational model to benefit your employees and customers.

Introduction

Remotely Possible will introduce you to scenarios that predate the Internet, the Covid-19 pandemic, and speak to the fact that people who wanted to work together while separated by geography have always found ways to do so. You will read about specific examples from various organizations and learn about the concepts and practices you should consider as you embrace the possibility of transforming your workplace into a truly remote, distributed, potentially asynchronous, productive, and satisfying organization.

The book will combine best practices from experiential and academic perspectives with practical examples and case studies where appropriate.

Lessons from a Pandemic

Remote Work Works

In 1918, World War I was coming to an end. A global pandemic that no one alive today remembers was also ravaging the world, accelerated by returning soldiers and resumption of commerce that had been impacted by the war years. Much like the Covid-19 pandemic of 2020, the Spanish Flu pandemic took a heavy toll of lives and had a tremendous impact on societies around the world as people and institutions struggled to cope with the effects and long-term outcomes.

As with the 2020 Covid-19 pandemic, the 1918 Spanish Flu forced businesses around the world to shut down or significantly curtail their operations. Since most businesses were manufacturing-based, many businesses were forced to close due to illnesses and fear of contracting or spreading the virus. In the United States, economic activity was impacted even though the closures ordered were not as widespread as those experienced in the 2020 Covid-19 pandemic due to the continued efforts to fight World War I (Bodenhorn, 2020).

In 1918, the manufacturing-oriented nature of business and industry as well as the relative newness of global communication meant remote work was not an option for most organizations. Despite the existence of trans-oceanic telegraph and emergence of wireless communications during World War I, these technologies were not widely adopted to the point where they could have realistically been used to enable non-manufacturing personnel to work remotely. Nor was it common for business tools to be anywhere but in offices, factories, or other places of business. Yet, it is likely that even then, a few enterprising businesses found ways to operate remotely.

In 1918, manufacturing was much more local than it is now. Factories and other businesses were embedded in the community, not in a business or technology park on the edge of town or in city-center offices to such an extent. Light manufacturing was often conducted at home as piece work (mostly by women and children). A classic example is the making of matches, but there are many others. Many more people worked in agriculture as well. This is not to say that remote working was widespread; rather, it points to a different societal and work model than exists in the 21st century.

Note In the 21st century we take the existence of technology enablers and remote work for granted. The opening paragraphs serve to remind us that this has not always been the case – it certainly was not in 1918 during the Spanish Flu pandemic.

Fast-Forward – 21st Century Enablers

The rapid expansion of ever-faster global communication systems throughout the 20th century, especially the emergence of the Internet as a communication and commerce network, put businesses and workers of the 20th and 21st centuries in very different places than their counterparts of the 1918 Spanish flu pandemic. The near-ubiquitous availability of Internet access to businesses and workers around the globe and the leveling and commoditization of Internet access and related systems put the possibility for effective and consistent remote work in the hands of almost anyone with a computer and a reasonably reliable Internet connection.

21st century knowledge workers and information-based businesses realized they could recruit and deploy a workforce made of qualified people no matter their geographic location. Physical location and borders became less and less of an issue as the Internet and various enabling software platforms and business models evolved through the first two decades of the century. Even as remote and distributed work scenarios expanded and became more and more commonplace, opposing perspectives questioned the efficacy of remote workers as well as the impact on collaboration compared to colocated workforces. Some Theory X leaders and their organizations questioned how workers could be trusted to be productive when not physically observed, absent the Hawthorne Effect to ensure their productivity. More forward-thinking leaders in start-up companies built their organizations as remote companies from the start, focused on people as the key to making it work.

Communication and collaboration tools emerged to make distributed team collaboration easier – some efficient, some not so much. Internet Relay Chat (IRC) enabled geographically distributed teams to communicate via text in real time. Tools like Skype added improved user interfaces (UI) and combined Voice Over Internet Protocol (VOIP) capabilities to enable anyone to place calls and instant message. Tools like GitHub enabled remote teams of software developers to store and manage code. Emerging cloud storage firms like Dropbox and Box provided distributed organizations with the ability to store and share files in the cloud.

Salesforce was founded in 1999. While not the first Software as a Service (SaaS) company, Salesforce was the first to gain traction and market share through aggressive marketing and sales tactics intended to enable business users to bypass their IT departments and host salesforce automation (SFA) and customer relationship management (CRM) in the cloud, further enabling remote organizations. Salesforce rapidly added capabilities through development and acquisitions, providing more business operational capabilities to distributed organizations while expanding on this operating model themselves. Salesforce provided a successful model for other SaaS companies to emulate, and themselves created an ecosystem on which similar companies control products that would enable remote distributed work and commerce.

Slack (which as of this writing is likely to become part of Salesforce in 2021) introduced a collaboration platform in 2013 that rapidly gained traction, especially with technical and creative organizations. At CloudCraze (a software company where I worked from 2012 - 2017), our product development teams experimented and rapidly adopted Slack for our distributed software development and delivery operations. So quickly did this tool become the de facto standard for remote synchronous and asynchronous communication that other part of the business such as sales and marketing felt left out.

I was impressed by the rapid organic adoption and quick organization around this tool. Clearly, others were as well, since Slack saw rapid adoption and growth from 2013 on. By the time of the Covid-19 pandemic in 2020, organizations using Slack and similar tools such as Teams and Zoom had some remote collaboration tools as well as basic or even maturing practices for their use in place – and not a moment too soon. Starting in March of 2020, tools like Zoom, Teams, Slack, WebEx, Google Meet would become a backbone of communication and collaboration as the world's workforces went remote.

Remote Work Works

From the mid-1990s through this writing (which I started in mid-2020), remote and distributed teams have proven to be effective scenarios for teams I've led, coached or worked on, delivering technology and knowledge projects successfully around the globe. Countless organizations leverage remote distributed teams to grow, succeed and deliver using the skills and capabilities of motivated remote workforces, with people and teams distributed across countries and the world.

Many of the examples I refer to in this book come from a variety of my personal experiences as a team member and as a leader or manager working in remote or distributed team situations. Other examples come from project management and change leadership courses I have taught that include components of leading and managing remote and geographically distributed teams. Still other examples come from countless conversations and debates about the effectiveness of remote and distributed teams that I have had with colleagues, students, and other leaders.

My first experience on a remote team was in 1993. Our customer was consumer products giant Proctor & Gamble, and we were continuing work on a successful custom hazardous materials training program that had been launched the previous year. My colleague Susan and I were technical writers at J. J. Keller & Associates of Neenah, Wisconsin. Susan was a really good technical writer who had also managed a couple of early projects for what would eventually become Keller Custom Solutions. Susan's husband had decided to go back into the military, and we wanted to keep working with Susan. I took over the project management role for this project and for future custom projects, and Susan moved out to the East Coast so her husband could fly helicopters for the U.S. Marines.

Susan was extremely talented and efficient at developing manuscripts and doing research. As we landed new clients and continued work for existing clients, Susan and I met at client sites and then exchanged material via FedEx and fax, until we both got email accounts and could send smaller files as attachments over our 14.4 modems. With only a few minor glitches due primarily to the occasional hurricane, Susan and I completed numerous projects together working as a distributed team.

As J. J. Keller's custom solutions capability evolved, we developed video productions, publications, and computer-based training for clients around the United States. This often involved developing content with team members located in various cities and collaborating via phone, fax, FedEx, and slow dial-up Internet. Before high-speed Internet enabled rapid transmission of software work in progress, many Friday afternoons were spent burning work in progress software or demos to CD-ROMs in order to make the last

FedEx shipment of the day and get it into the hands of the client or another team member by Monday morning,

These experiences with capable and dedicated people at this point early in my professional career showed me that working with the best people no matter where they were located was a model that worked, and I have never stopped believing in that lesson.

Note For the remainder of the book, the phrase "Remote" or "Remote Teams" will be interspersed with "Distributed or Virtual Teams" wherever possible. One of the points I'll make later is how critical it is to ensure that everyone feels and has the same experience. Use of the word "Remote" seems to discourage that effect.

Remote Stumbles

Countless organizations around the world were using distributed teams and workers quite successfully prior to 2020. IBM, Yahoo, Salesforce, Microsoft, Automattic, and Google are just a few examples – although under CEO Marissa Mayer, Yahoo significantly curtailed the remote work practice. IBM dialed it back as well. Mayer's rationale was for Yahoo to have more of the serendipitous unplanned "hallway encounters" that she believed led to creativity and innovation. According to Bill Davidow writing for *The Atlantic* in 2013, Mayer had no choice but to end remote work options because she needed to rescue Yahoo's culture in order to make Yahoo competitive again, and that could not be accomplished, according to Davidow, *because Mayer did not know how to build a winning culture with people working remotely* (Davidow, 2013). IBM's reasons for ending long-standing and much-touted remote work arrangements were similar, the thinking being that more collaboration would increase the pace of work. But in the view of some mid-career workers, many who had built their lives around IBM's decades-old remote work policy, IBM's rationale for curtailing remote work had nothing to do with spontaneous collaboration and innovation and everything to do with cutting headcount (Simmons, 2017).

A third organization, Best Buy, also chose to end a remote work policy, citing competition and wanting everyone back in the office. Before ending the program, Best Buy's policy of remote work and evaluating employees purely on performance had gained much notice, and the creators of the program had even opened a consulting firm based on the concepts underpinning Best Buy's program. Criticism of this decision focused on Best Buy's decision in a crisis and under new management to take a step backwards in leadership approach (Nisen, 2013).

A quick assessment of these three examples reveals a common theme – all three of these corporate giants were struggling when they made the decision to end remote work policies. Yahoo was losing to Google, IBM was flailing and seeing their stock price pummeled, and Best Buy was also struggling. Looking back at the decision to revoke remote work policies, IBM surrendered around $100 million in office space savings while Best Buy gave up a workforce cohort that saw 45% less turnover compared to their in-office counterparts. How did this change in remote work policy turn out? Yahoo was acquired, IBM's fortunes continued to decline, while Best Buy has changed its business model to be less reliant on in-store sales (Sarabyn, 2020). It is not likely that ending remote work options had any contribution to slowing the slides of these respective companies.

Becoming Remotely Successful

I attended an excellent seminar at the 2011 Project Management Institute's North American conference in Dallas that featured a presentation from an agile software development team working in a distributed model across every time zone on the globe. The presenters described how they used instant messaging tools and cloud-based tools for collaboration and code storage. They described how they shared the inconvenience of midnight and early morning meeting times so that no team or team member was always losing sleep by attending 2 am conference calls. This approach to work resonated with me and was influential in my early 2012 career change to a company that was using this model.

Automattic (maker of WordPress) is well-known for its distributed teams culture. This culture and their practices are documented in Scott Berkun's 2013 book *The Year Without Pants*. Berkun describes a culture in which distributed teams are the norm and baked into Automattic's DNA. He describes how periodic gatherings reinforced the connections and culture. The Automattic example and my own experience at CloudCraze Software shows how companies not only leverage distributed teams but were built from Day 1 as fully distributed companies.

Matt Mullenweg, founder of Automattic, was likely not surprised to see much of the world adopt and adapt to remote work. Interviewed in July 2020, Mullenweg expressed admiration for how quickly many organizations pivoted to remote work (Gelles, 2020). A promoter and advocate of remote work since founding Automattic in 2005, Mullenweg describes five levels of autonomy in distributed work and professed that most organizations adapted to the 2020 pandemic at a level two – replicating their on-site work practices and operating in asynchronous mode while using technology to enable communication and collaboration in real-time. Later we'll look more closely at Mullenweg's five-level model of autonomous work (Mullenweg, 2020).

At CloudCraze in 2012, we were proving that remote work worked as we scaled up our product and delivery practices from a single small team to multiple client delivery teams and a larger product development team. Our distributed product development team leveraged agile practices, instant messaging, and cloud-based development and storage systems to deliver evolving releases of our ecommerce product. We held our scrum standup meetings on Mondays, Wednesdays, and Fridays using Go2Meeting as the conferencing platform. Our expanding delivery teams joined in from our client sites as we launched new projects. When we weren't at client sites or making periodic visits to the Deerfield, IL office, we all worked from our respective home offices in cities across the United States as we worked to expand and improve the product as well as deliver modern ecommerce client implementations.

I have vivid memories of virtual daily standups that I initiated from New York City and Charlottesville, Virginia, throughout 2012 and 2013. One of my most challenging series of virtual standups happened nightly at 6 p.m. in the lobby of a hotel in Berlin while we completed final development and user testing of an ecommerce deployment for Coca-Cola Germany as well as prepared for an important release of our product prior to that year's edition of Dreamforce, the extravagant annual conference hosted in San Francisco by Salesforce (prior to 2020).

With key members of the product team joining the client delivery team in Berlin and with others located in the United States, we collaborated remotely to complete both the Coca-Cola Germany implementation as well as our critical product release prior to this major and visible product conference.

We did similar work with a client implementation in Bangkok. After the initial kick-off visits were complete, we placed two key team members with the client in Bangkok (see Figure 1-1) and continued our development and delivery work remotely from the United States. Daily conference calls with our Bangkok team and client were scheduled so that the local Thai custom of delayed morning arrival and late nights aligned with availability of the US team. We had previously honed similar practices to work effectively with our clients and delivery teams working in Brussels and Berlin, so adding Bangkok to our plate of remote teams was not much of a stretch.

Figure 1-1. Colleagues confer with a client at a remote project kickoff

Through the second decade of the 2000s, the success of companies and products like Slack, WordPress, CloudCraze, and many others proved that remote distributed organizational models were not only possible but highly effective catalysts for growth and success. CloudCraze, one of many emerging product companies built on the Salesforce cloud ecosystem, had proven successful enough that in August 2015 we were acquired by a group of Chicago-based investors.

By November 2015 we were almost done with a release of the product we'd been working on all summer and fall. The timing was perfect to bring our distributed development teams together in Chicago to complete the release and build relationships within the newly organized development and support team structure. As vice-president of development and support, the planning and performance of this on-site meeting was my responsibility.

Prior to that November 2015 on-site, several members of the product development team had never met each other in person! Although some had met in various company meetings and at client delivery locations through the evolving years, some newer to the quality assurance and support teams had joined the company and worked exclusively from locations like Florida, Northern California, and Utah, and this team meeting in Chicago was a first.

One of the reasons a full-team on-site meeting like this was such a big deal was because the product team had been working successfully in their distributed remote model – such meetings were not typical. They happened periodically with team leads for strategic planning, and ad hoc when the executives, team leads, and developers found themselves gathered at client locations for kick-offs and go-lives. The previous major on-site gathering had taken place with CloudCraze executives and team leads in Captiva Island, Florida in November 2014. After a particularly successful year, the founder and CEO wanted to combine a week of review and strategic planning with celebrations in this beautiful location. It was a memorable week capping a successful year of remote work.

The CloudCraze examples I have shared are important to the whole premise of the book – as this book evolves, I will refer periodically to examples from CloudCraze and how, after successful building years, the new owners had very different viewpoints of distributed remote teams, their effectiveness, and their contribution to company culture. I use these examples to illustrate models of successful remote distributed teamwork as well as to illustrate practices and behaviors that are detrimental to the culture and success of remote distributed organizations.

Note The stories you've just reviewed are a few examples of how remote work worked prior to 2020. Organizations around the globe ran successful distributed teams and projects prior to the Covid-19 pandemic. The pandemic forced many organizations to try remote work options.

2020 – Covid-19 Forces a Global Experiment

In late February 2020 I was CIO at a large technical college in south-central Wisconsin, but I was working remotely from Tucson, Arizona for a couple of weeks. After spending part of the afternoon at the University of Arizona campus, my wife and I were having a drink in downtown Tucson. I took a few minutes to check my email. One of the listservs I belonged to was blowing up with fellow higher ed CIOs discussing early actions their campuses were taking to deal with an evolving virus that the world would come to know as Covid-19. I sent an email to my provost and a VP at my college, recommending that we meet as soon as possible to discuss responses.

Similar conversations were taking place around the globe as news came out of China and other countries and Covid-19 rapidly became a global pandemic. Cities and countries went into lockdowns and organizations around the world sent their workers home. Colleges, universities, and schools sent their students and faculty home. With no warning whatsoever, the world was forced into an experiment to see if distributed workers, teams, and organizations could operate effectively.

At my college, we handed out laptops and Internet hotspots to students, faculty, and staff to enable classes and operations to continue. Many organizations around the globe took similar steps, and the global supply of laptops, webcams, headsets, and other peripherals needed by suddenly distributed workers and teams was quickly depleted. Although the Internet and many cloud-based storage and collaboration tools initially staggered under the sudden weight of shifting businesses and teaching at all levels to a fully online model, providers quickly adjusted and added capacity and features to sustain and support this sudden shift.

In developed nations, the inequities present in socioeconomic and technology resources were made even more evident. As someone fortunate to have worked in remote models for over a decade, and with access to technology and a well-equipped home office, the pivot to remote work was nothing new to me. Colleagues of mine shared stories of retreating to quiet places in northern Wisconsin with their families in order to ride out the initial weeks and months of the first lockdowns. Analysis of cell phone usage and related data showed patterns of migration from the wealthiest parts of New York City to locations in upstate New York as well as Florida, while lower income residents were forced to stay put and ride out the lockdown (Quealy, 2020).

Areas like San Francisco and the Silicon Valley of the United States saw an exodus of employees moving to rural locations and other states as their densely packed urban office spaces closed. The cloud-based technical nature of work in many of these companies was one of the key factors that enabled fully remote distributed workforces. Not only did this prove a critical capability for these organizations to continue operating, but the sudden taste of life outside of crowded and expensive San Francisco and Silicon Valley showed many workers that remote life outside the city was a better fit for themselves and their families, and that San Francisco and Silicon Valley costs were not a requirement to developing good products.

Distributed Equals Risk Management

Some organizations didn't miss a beat – they were already wired for such a scenario and just kept operating. Ars Technica, a technically-oriented news site, ran stories describing their distributed work culture and how 20 years of operating this way made the pandemic lockdown just another day in the (home) office (Hutchinson, 2020). All around the world, other organizations rapidly discovered what many already knew: a distributed workforce provided some measure of risk mitigation in the face of a rapidly spreading virus. Whether it's a global pandemic or the seasonal influenza, a distributed workforce helps reduce the risk that illness will spread across an organization.

The risk mitigation benefits of a distributed workforce and teams is not limited to stopping the spread of illnesses. In 2018 and 2020, two horrific instances of workplace gun violence in my state helped drive home another point – if an organization experiences an event of any kind that shuts down a location, distributed workers and teams remain largely unaffected – at least physically. Weather, maintenance and construction events, large gatherings, and civil unrest all pose threats to location-based organizations. Distributed teams and workers mitigate these risks.

While I was the vice-president of development and support at CloudCraze Software (now part of Salesforce), one of my responsibilities was writing a business continuity and disaster recovery plan. Since we were 100% cloud-based with our product as well as our IT systems, our continuity and disaster recovery plans mainly consisted of "go remote, go distributed, resume working." With a cloud-first IT model and a distributed versus colocated workforce, organizations can mitigate risks that are associated with large workforces located in single, large physical locations with on-premise IT systems.

Note Distributed remote workforces and systems mitigate risks associated with people and systems concentrated in physical locations.

As I noted earlier, I was the CIO of Madison College in Madison, Wisconsin when the pandemic hit. Our leadership team discussed the evolving pandemic with greater and greater urgency throughout February. By early March we were making plans to pivot to a completely remote model of teaching, learning, and campus operations. We were fortunate that previous investments in technology infrastructure and architecture enabled our college, with its large urban footprint in Madison and four regional campuses in south-central Wisconsin, to pivot to a remote model and provide equipment and connectivity to our students, faculty, and staff.

Some faculty had previously resisted online teaching and learning and needed significant training and support in order to make this move. Other faculty were leading-edge early adopters and able to make the all-online model work quickly and effectively. Staff across the college rapidly learned how to perform their work as distributed teams. We had been piloting cloud-based collaboration and storage systems, and these pilots provided immediate value as we were forced to do all of our meeting and collaboration using these tools. Areas of our college became expert resources for other colleagues less familiar with these tools and helped everyone reach a level of usage that supported effective remote and distributed operations.

The lesson that emerged from our quick pivot to a remote, distributed regional campus operation was that our business systems and distributed infrastructure had given us a significant measure of risk management that we were able to immediately leverage to continue operating effectively. Many other organizations experienced similar success, while others struggled due to poor planning, resistant cultures, and lack of technology resources.

As noted, workers and companies in places like San Francisco, Silicon Valley, and other crowded and pricey urban locations began to experience a different lifestyle working remotely from rural locations and in less expensive cities and states. Some progressive companies communicated to their employees, customers, and the media that, in many cases, remote work would become a long-term or permanent option. As we will discuss in later chapters, this is a smart move. Not only does it embody the risk management aspects of a distributed workforce, but it helps with long-term employee satisfaction, helps with recruiting, and can lower operating costs by avoiding pricey commercial real estate.

As well, some companies realized they did not need to offer the premium salaries necessary to attract the best workers in expensive cities. The trade-off for some workers to stay in bucolic remote locations was to accept a drop in salary, since the high cost of living was no longer a justification for the higher salary. For some, the opportunity to trade higher salaries for more living space, less density, and lower cost of living was a good move. This is a potentially touchy topic and trade-off – not all organizations can or should tie salaries to location when building a distributed workforce.

Summary

This introductory chapter has shared lessons from the Covid-19 pandemic which, for many organizations, was their first experiment with distributed remote work. For many other organizations, this experience was just further proof that their remote model and workforce was effective and provided them with significant flexibility, adaptability, and risk management when an unforeseen and catastrophic global event occurred.

This chapter introduced a few examples of products and organizations that either enable remote distributed work or were successful as a direct result of adopting and evolving a remote distributed organizational model. In future chapters, I will refer to these examples and share stories to illustrate important points on how remote work is not only possible, but also an ideal and successful model for many organizations.

In the next chapter we will discuss some elements of remote work that we already knew. We'll talk about how finding the best people wherever they live helps organizations build successful distributed teams and organizations. We will talk about real estate – the decision to acquire and pay for expensive office space is a critical decision for any organization. We will discuss how thoughtful planning and deliberate adoption of a distributed organizational model can help avoid the expense of real estate and provide greater flexibility for organizations to grow, innovate, adapt, and succeed. We will also note that costs and lost time due to travel can also be significantly reduced in remote and distributed scenarios.

CHAPTER 2

Things We Knew

Location Matters

Bill Loumpouridis came out of the .com bust of the early 2000s with a couple of key goals: find work to earn a living and build a new kind of technology consulting company. Bill had departed one of the largest of the Chicago-area boutique web development firms prior to one of the largest implosions of that era and was determined not to repeat the mistakes that he had seen there both in terms of the business model as well as hiring and working with people and teams.

Bill came out of that experience and the .com implosion with a mantra for his own consulting firm – delivery excellence. Another key realization – one that would shape the culture of his new venture – was that he could and would leverage technology to hire the best people no matter where they lived. Bill called his new firm EDL Consulting – the EDL represented "**E**xcellence in **D**elivery **L**eadership."

> **Note** The theme "hire the best people wherever they are" is core to making remote work possible and successful and reoccurs in examples throughout the book.

Hire the Best Wherever They Are

It has been possible and practical for well over two decades to hire someone to work in your organization that lives on the other side of the country or

Chapter 2 | Things We Knew

even the other side of the world. In the EDL example, founder Bill Loumpouridis leveraged that model to build a successful consulting company headquartered in Chicago and with staff all over the United States. When I joined in January 2012, my new boss was working from Kansas. Members of the ecommerce team that I would work with were based in California, Texas, Georgia, Chicago, Minnesota, Utah, Kentucky, Pennsylvania, and other places I've since forgotten.

My first taste of the EDL Consulting remote distributed model was during the interview process. I drove to EDL's small corporate office in Deerfield, IL (more on offices and real estate choices later) for my in-person interviews with some of the team who worked locally. Aside from a lunch interview with Bill, the most important interview was with my potential new boss, Rob. Rob was the VP of the ecommerce practice and was interviewing me via Skype from his home office in Kansas. We had a good conversation that must have made a favorable impression on Rob, and I was hired. Once I started, I'd be working remotely from my home in Madison with a new team distributed across the United States as described, and with clients also located across the country and eventually around the globe.

This story illustrates the start of my own personal example of my first experience with an all-virtual company, founded from day one on the principles of a remote workforce. Companies like Automattic, Collage, Venafi, Kuali, InVision, and Aha! are just a few examples of organizations that build their business model and culture on the knowledge that they can hire the best people to join their company regardless of where they were physically located. This principle enables any company to be more competitive in the fierce fight to attract and retain top talent in the technical fields and other fields necessary to grow your business and succeed.

As a founder, recruiter, or hiring manager, the knowledge that your geographic recruiting area is unlimited is incredibly powerful and incredibly liberating. You can go after the best talent you can find, and that talent might be interested in joining you because there are no requirements to move for the job or limitations on where they work. Talents who have roots or family in a particular city or area but have an interest in working for an organization in another part of the country (or world) have no restrictions in where they look for work or what organization they join in an all-remote structure.

As the firm grew and expanded coming into 2009, EDL Consulting spun out a software product company called CloudCraze. The product had been an organic internal startup based on a realization that there was a niche for business-to-business (B2B) ecommerce on the rapidly expanding Salesforce ecosystem and platform. As CloudCraze grew, gaining customers and notoriety, so did its need for talent beyond the core founding development staff. People like Ummy (Austin, TX), John (Pasadena, CA), Thomas (Atlanta, GA), Matt (Provo, UT), Andrew (Lexington, KY) came aboard to build out the core development and support team. Whether building the product software or implementing the new commerce system and supporting our clients, this small, core distributed team had a growing and successful product on its hands.

In mid-2013, Bill realized we needed dedicated quality assurance staff to review and test the functionality and quality of new features and to regression test the existing software platform to a degree of depth and a speed beyond our capabilities. He reached out to a team of software testers he knew of located in various cities in California. As will be noted at multiple points in this book, that group of QA testers worked remotely, and it wasn't until November 2015 that they met the CloudCraze team or other members of the software development team in person.

Once again, the remote model that Bill had embraced at the start of the business enabled EDL, just like it enables any organization built on this principle, to find the people that we needed to respond to demands for particular talent and to scale the business rapidly without significant geographic limitations on finding and hiring people. Companies like Automattic (WordPress) and Collage.com have followed similar principles to start, build, and successfully scale their companies.

In the case of Collage.com, founders Joe Golden and Kevin Borders grew their company from just themselves working part-time in 2010 to a team of 45 remote, home-based people by 2016. They made a conscious decision not to establish a physical "home office." Instead, they hired people who had the interest, aptitude, and ability to work remotely, and they developed business practices that enabled and facilitated a distributed organization. Joe Golden based the decision on more than just a gut feeling – a section of his PhD dissertation assessed the effect of non-compensation elements of a job (such as the ability to work remotely), and internal surveys of Collage.com staff confirmed that the culture and productivity of Collage.com reflected the outcomes of other studies and research findings: Remote and home-based workforces were as or more productive than those that had to come into an office to work (Stanton and Ghosh, 2016).

A 2016 Harvard Business School case study examines Golden and Borders' perspectives on remote work models as part of the overall study. Quoted in the case study, Borders noted that in addition to reducing office politics as a factor, "exceptional people" often look only for remote jobs. When a family matter or other issue necessitates that a person move, that person can keep right on working with the company wherever they need or want to live. This capability is very important to small and growing firms, where there may not be other similarly trained staff ready, willing and able to step into a role vacated by a departing employee (Stanton and Ghosh, 2016).

WordPress is the most popular web authoring and content management tool on the planet. WordPress is one of the several products in the product portfolio of Automattic, the company founded by Matt Mullenweg in 2005.

Like EDL's and Collage.com's founders, Automattic's Mullenweg decided that a distributed organization would be in the DNA of the company from the beginning. Also, like EDL and Collage, Automattic was (and is) able to hire the best people for a role, regardless of their location. Former Microsoft program manager Scott Berkun discusses this capability and practice in his book *The Year Without Pants*. Calling "indifference to physical location a fundamental assumption of how the company is organized and managed", Berkun outlines how this enables Automattic to "hire the best talent in the world, wherever they are" (Berkun, 2013).

Berkun described the interview process for a remote candidate joining the WordPress team – since your work will be done wherever you are, the interview is simply a chance to prove you can do the work through a trial assignment. No flying, no overnights – just a meaningful chance to show that you can do the work, right from where you are (Berkun, 2013). As of this writing, Automattic's "About Us" page notes 1310 "Automatticians" working in 77 countries and speaking 96 different languages (Automattic, 2020). Clearly, Automattic has remained committed to and has been very successful with their founding philosophy – hire the best people wherever they are.

Let the People Work and Live Where They Want

When the Covid-19 pandemic hit in March 2020, Madison College had a mix of full-time staff and consultants all working on-site at our Madison campus. Our PeopleSoft consultants flew in from all over the country on a regular basis. We put an immediate stop to that as more data about the Covid-19 pandemic and the necessity to curtail travel became clear. This actually worked out quite well for the consultants, who had been asking if they could work remotely even before the pandemic struck. As our entire IT department along with the rest of the college left our campus and went home to work, some of our full-time staff left Madison to join family in places throughout Wisconsin and throughout the country. Some took the opportunity just to live and work someplace new and different while the pandemic evolved.

As a long-time advocate for a distributed workforce and for allowing remote working arrangements, I had already been working with my leadership team on some basic remote work guidelines, since the concept of "teleworking" was new to the college. Before February 2020, my leadership team was tentatively prepared to dip their toe in the remote work water, so to speak. The pandemic forced us to experiment successfully with distributed teams within IT and throughout the entire institution. Overall, our technology teams did not miss a beat in supporting the college's transition to remote work even while we were maintaining and expanding our own technology capabilities for the college's new remote working and teaching scenarios.

A couple of months into the transition to an all-remote work model, we had team members working quite happily throughout the state and in some instances, around the country. The leader of our learning management system team had decamped to Texas to be closer to her daughters. One member of our security team found a place in northern Wisconsin that brought him joy and enabled him to work in peace and tranquility. One executive even sold his house in Madison and relocated for several months to work from a mountain state.

As was the case for organizations around the world, the Covid-19 pandemic that started in 2020 was a jarring and unfortunate experience, but it also reinforced some things that many other organizations already knew: Talented, motivated people can work from anywhere given the opportunity, given trust, the right tools, and a culture that rewards the results achieved versus the time spent in the office.

Remote and Distributed Enables Diversity

2020 was not just a year of a pandemic. Shocking events in the United States during 2020 also sparked an intense focus on social justice and racial injustices along with renewed and sustained attention to increasing the diversity of organizations and teams. At Madison College, the success of remote work gave me the opportunity to leverage and advocate for this as a means and an opportunity to increase the diversity of our technology team. Knowing that we could recruit technical talent from around the country in addition to the greater Madison area meant that we could have more opportunities to recruit and hire and retain a more diverse workforce.

We know from experience and research that diversity in the organization improves the capabilities and performance of teams and organizations by introducing diversity of thinking, backgrounds, and lived experiences. The remote and distributed work model enables organizations to increase the diversity of their workforce by recruiting across a much larger geographic scope than they would otherwise have if they limited themselves to an on premise, locally defined working and recruiting model.

The interview process itself is also streamlined in that, like the Automattic example earlier in this chapter, the entire interview process as well as onboarding and start-up takes place remotely. This makes it easier for candidates to participate in interviews and removes potential hardships some candidates might face when trying to arrange a chance to interview for a new, better job. Travel is potentially eliminated, and less time off from a current job or other obligations is needed to participate in the interview.

Diversity in the workforce should be an ongoing concern and objective of every organization, and discarding the geographic limitations imposed by an "in-office only" working model enables organizations to act upon diversity as a value, to the benefit and advantage of the organization, its people, and the community.

Real Estate Is Expensive

Bill Loumpouridis and I were having dinner one night at the Kinzie Chophouse in downtown Chicago prior to heading to the Chicago Theater to see our client, Neil Young, perform solo in concert (Neil Young's Pono audio product features in future examples later in the book). As we ate, Bill reflected and told some stories about the early days of EDL Consulting. It happened that his earliest office was located just a few blocks from the restaurant. We're talking about some pricey downtown Chicago real estate here. At some point in the evolution of EDL, Bill must have reconsidered how the cost of downtown Chicago real estate factored into his financial models as well as quality of life calculations.

When I joined EDL/CloudCraze in 2012, the firm was located in Deerfield, IL. Far less expensive than downtown Chicago real estate, the space had offices for the small on-site local staff, but with fully equipped hoteling desks for any remote staff who might be in the office at any given time. A suitably equipped and sized conference room enabled client meetings and internal strategy and planning meetings. Bill had clearly decided what elements did and did not bring value to his distributed organizational model. As well, the Deerfield office was a few steps from a METRA line and had comfortable accommodations for visiting staff a short walk across the street. Lastly, Deerfield was close to Bill's home in a quiet nearby suburb.

Fast-forward to a huge location change driven by very different considerations and motivations. When CloudCraze (which was founded from inside EDL) was acquired by a group of three Chicago investors called Aktion Partners in August 2015, one of their first moves was to relocate CloudCraze to downtown Chicago offices. At first, we occupied a set of disconnected office suites on the 22nd floor. By summer 2016, a beautiful new and modern space had been remodeled on the second floor overlooking Wacker Drive, and CloudCraze moved in. The space was the epitome of the open, industrial look that was and still is de rigueur for high-tech and software companies. It was an impressive office space and certainly wowed our clients, partners, and potential investors. This was not an inexpensive endeavor, as our new CEO enjoyed pointing out.

It was also a total reversal and pivot from the culture and philosophy of CloudCraze's founders and this change quickly had a negative impact on the morale of the remote team. In a very short period of time, a culture divide began to emerge between the downtown Chicago staff who basically worked 9 to 5 and the remote staff that worked from early in the morning until after midnight. More on this later.

Space Needs Flex with Remote Models

The remote work model offers growing or changing organizations many options and flexibility regarding their working space and its location. With some or all of the organization working from home or elsewhere, the space needs for the main office can be considerably reduced. If an organization feels a need for a prime location whether for image reasons or for entirely practical reasons, this space can be smaller and cheaper. Consider this – If you can forgo prime real estate in expensive locales and markets, you save on rent and can invest in people and technology – elements that might provide more return on investment than the spend on the physical space.

In the course of researching and writing this book, one of the interesting facts I learned about Automattic is that their San Francisco office closed in 2017, doubtless at least in part due to the cost of maintaining it compared to the use it got. Scott Berkun described how during his time with Automattic the office was seldom occupied – a tribute to the Automatic culture and the success of the remote work model (Berkun, 2013). Coming out of the Covid-19 pandemic, many organizations planning to embrace remote work for the long haul made important decisions regarding their office real estate needs. For example, Salesforce canceled a 325,000 square foot office space lease because its updated work policies anticipate that at least half of its workforce will work on remote and flexible schedules (McLean, 2021).

As you consider your organization's needs for space and the location options and costs associated with space, it behooves a leader to think seriously and carefully about your staff, your space needs, and how adopting remote and distributed models of working affects all of these elements. Make sure you consider the trade-offs between location, commute times, proximity to public transportation, existing employee locations, and of course, the cost of office space factoring in square footage and location.

Plan to Rethink Your Current Space

In early 2020, Madison College began demolition of my IT department spaces for a long-planned renovation. We'd spent a good portion of 2019 in planning and design meetings for this new space – it was exciting to think about how to make optimal use of what was sure to be a beautiful and modern new area, with all of the teams (previously parked in separate rooms) in one large space. During the planning process, all assumptions revolved around the need to accommodate about 110 "butts in seats" inclusive of full-time College IT staff and the consultants and student workers who made up the department.

The 2020 pandemic changed everything, including my thinking about this new space. As of this writing, we're rethinking the whole layout – with potentially half of the staff working elsewhere at any given time, do we need permanent desks for everyone, or can we switch to a combination of hoteling desks and flexible and configurable workspaces, along with some permanent cubicles for those staff who plan to be or need to be on-site most of the time? Do I, as CIO, need a private office reserved for my use even when not working remotely, since when I am working on-site, meetings tend to keep me away from my desk at least 50% of the time?

This type of thinking enabled our space and furniture design to offer back approximately 25% of our originally planned space to the college to use in addressing the challenging aspects of optimizing physical space for the evolving needs of a modern busy technical college even as we looked out to the post-Covid learning and working environment.

Starting out with or moving to a remote and distributed model means that space needs can be approached in a totally different way. I've personally never worked in an organization that had enough meeting spaces. When you do have people on-site, the most likely reason is because they want to meet and collaborate in person with other humans – this means meeting space, not offices and desks. If you need or decide to have physical office space, having a majority of your team working offsite most of the time means that space can be dedicated to meeting and collaborative space. Trust me – your organization will be more productive and will thank you or whoever makes this decision.

A variation on this thinking and the many options available in office furniture configurations means that physical space can be designed in a flexible, configurable, and collaborative way. Temporary collaboration or project team spaces can be created using large movable whiteboard panels and rolling movable desks. Project teams and cross-functional groups can form temporary colocation spaces defined by the movable whiteboards, and then reconfigure this furniture and the spaces when needs change.

A *Harvard Business Review* article by Anne - Laure Fayard, John Weeks and Mahwesh Khan theorizes that the modern office space should account for the mix of remote and on-site work that will be the norm in the 2020s and beyond. The article notes the social components that have always been an important part of the work experience, and introduces us to the concept of the office as a *culture space*:

> *providing workers with a social anchor, facilitating connections, enabling learning, and fostering unscripted, innovative collaboration (Fayard, et al., 2021).*

How do you arrive at the optimal mix of space for a projected on-site and off-site workforce? Assuming you are moving to this model from on always in-office model, start with your assumptions and do some surveys. Consider elements such as

- How many staff do you anticipate in the office more than two days a week?
- What kind of space do you need for people and teams to be most productive?
- Does your culture embrace or resist shared desks and hoteling models?
- How do people commute to the workplace?
- How long will they stay?
- Do you have systems in place to efficiently enable people to reserve hoteling desks for days they are in the office?
- Does it make sense to build flexible and configurable spaces to accommodate scenarios you have not envisioned?

Make sure you are thinking about the plug and play set-ups that should be at every shared space so that staff coming in for a day have monitors, keyboards, and places to store their backpacks and personal belongings. Make sure you have the means to schedule these spaces so people can reserve them for days they come into the office. We should always be thinking about minimizing exposure to seasonal viruses – consider arranging for the cleaning and disinfecting of shared workspaces both by their daily users as well as by custodial staff, if applicable.

Remember when planning and designing space that it is easier to turn meeting space into temporary desk space than the other way around. Periodic influxes of remote staff for planning meetings, collaborative problem-solving sessions, or company events may require that the meeting rooms turn into temporary team rooms or overflow desk space for a short period of time – design flexible and configurable spaces and furnish them accordingly.

We know that a good chunk of offices and desk spaces in the traditional workplace setting goes unused regardless of remote workforces. Vacations, meetings, flex schedules, and other absences mean that people are often away from their desks. One 2018 assessment offered that up to 40% of a workplace's dedicated desk space could be unused at any given time (Pochepan, 2018). Organizations adopting remote/distributed models can take this into account as they plan new or updated workspaces.

I'll not attempt to write a primer on calculating space utilization models – there is a lot of literature on this topic available, and the office furniture companies are all over it. It has in fact been my experience that whatever the emerging trends are in office space and furniture design, you can count on them being *behind* it. In reviewing available information and considering conversations with the facility planners in my own organization, key factors are clearly elements such as weekly utilization. Consider your approach and focus on elements such as overall space occupancy or individual desk usage. One consideration is the thought that a full-time on-prem person translates to 1:1 desk to staff ratio while 1:5 ratio of five remote workers using the same desk one day per week – both of these scenarios equate to 100% usage of that desk (Sheynkman, 2020).

Consider the Humans

When considering and designing for a hybrid workforce, there are human factors to consider such as proximity, need for personal space, feelings of safety, and other basic elements. The balance between creating sufficient space for shared or hoteling desks and the standard equipment expected to be in place while creating enough of those spaces to meet the anticipated numbers of humans expected to use these spaces is an art and a science. Humans can objectively understand the concept of temporary shared desk space and the relatively spartan nod given to personal privacy and space, and yet viscerally need some degree of separation in order to embrace these spaces and be productive. This is why for years, one could walk into an open concept office space and see dozens of people sitting side-by-side but wearing expensive noise-canceling headphones in order to preserve some sense of quiet, privacy, and concentration. So much for the constant collaboration the planners envisioned.

Expectations about workspace usage and methods to put in place some measure of control and certainty for the humans can be important. I recall walking into a San Francisco tech company a few years ago and seeing people literally sprawled all over the office – sitting back-to-back on lounge chairs, side-by-side at the coffee bar, parked in individual cubicles, and of course sitting at traditional open concept office desks. In the CloudCraze downtown Chicago space where I periodically worked, the local-to-Chicago crew tended to take the rows of closely spaced open concept desks at the front of the office overlooking Wacker Drive while the remote team and certain others ended up in the back room at similar desks – but with no windows.

In each case, the humans created traditions and unwritten rules about desks and space until the office administration stepped in to create rules. This is important to keep in mind. Many people need some sense of habit and certainty. For example, you may have a remote worker who decides to come in every Tuesday, and after a few weeks of securing the same desk space each Tuesday comes to think of that space as "theirs." Then one morning, they come in and find the space occupied by a smiling coworker, oblivious to the fact they have disrupted what has become a routine. It happened to me more than once.

The scheduling software which is embedded in all of our typical office productivity systems is one way to help alleviate this issue. Setting expectations for the people who are on-site most of the time and the remote team members who come in periodically can also help. Put the shared desk space and offices into the calendaring system and make it clear that the space should be scheduled according to one's on-site needs. Staff who are on-site three or more days per week could be given assigned desk space – I've seen that model work more than a few times.

In the Chicago/Wacker Drive example I referred to earlier, Heather, the office manager and admin to the CEO created a practice where the people who came into the office each day had assigned seats, and then reserved large blocks of space for people who came in from across the country on varying schedules. One private office was reserved for the use of remote executives when on-site.

Prior to the August 2015 move to downtown, Bill Loumpouridis and his EDL Consulting team in Deerfield had a similar set-up. One private office was reserved for Bill, who was in the office most days. The other private offices were scheduled by executives and managers as needed when in the office, sometimes by multiple people visiting and collaborating for much of the day. A shared desk space capable of accommodating about ten software development staff, equipped with monitors, adapters for Mac and PC laptops, and space for stuff occupied the open center of the floorplan. One modern and very well-equipped conference room with glass walls and one wall occupied by a giant glass whiteboard provided space for collaborative team meetings or for important client presentations and meetings.

Figure 2-1. The author's home office circa 2021

Devalue the Corner Office

In my career, I have had some good offices and some crappy offices and cubicles. The quality of my workspace has not always aligned with my title or tenure, and in some cases, despite the hourly rate my team and I were getting, the space we were allocated at the client's offices seemed intended to make us as unproductive as possible. These days, my favorite place to work is the current iteration of a home office my wife and I have shared since 2017 (see Figure 2-1).

Organizations say a lot about their culture with how they allocate offices and desk space. The founders of Intel famously did away with offices, opting for cubicles for everyone in the company, which was why you would find the world-famous Bob Noyce, Gordon Moore, and Andy Grove all working at cubicles. A bio-pharma company in Madison has a similar arrangement, with the exception that the founder and CEO uses an entire house as his office and meeting space – a holdover from when he lived in that house during the company's early days.

Fully remote organizations enable many different options and conversations about the design and allocation of physical space. Clearly, anyone who spends most of their time working from home or client locations does not need much square footage at an office.

As Matt Mullenweg (Automattic founder) notes, fully remote organizations enable every employee to design their own office experience while also removing the status that is often implied, intentionally or otherwise, through the location and size of a person's office. As Mullenweg noted in a 2020 *New York Times* interview with David Gelles:

> ...most people who choose to have offices are usually the bosses. And I've been to the offices of billionaire CEOs that have their own private bathroom, beautiful art and couches. But these are all things that you can have in your house. What I love about distributed organizations is that every single employee can have a corner office (Gelles, 2020).

In his own blog post shortly after this interview, Mullenweg goes on to describe the cultural differences between unlimited definitions of "office" or "workspace" as wherever you feel happiest and most productive (in my case that is often a local coffee shop or my screen porch as well as my home office desk) versus the variations of experiences between an entry-level person in a cubicle and most senior leaders in choice offices. Mullenweg points out that leaders may have conscious or unconscious biases based on their experience with their more desirable spaces that influence their thinking on culture and productivity in remote versus on-site work scenarios – be mindful of this potential bias (Mullenweg, 2020).

Business Travel – Spend Less, Invest More

Along with a reduction in the need for expense of real estate, models of remote work and distributed organizations also enable these organizations to spend far less on business travel. One emergent theme from the Covid-19 pandemic was the realization that many routine business meetings, whether internal or external, could be done without requiring travel to a physical location. This certainly has a positive impact through time savings and cost reductions for the people and companies not making the trip. Naturally, there is a cost to the many organizations who ordinarily profit from these trips – businesses such as conference organizers, airlines, hotels, and restaurants saw their revenue from conferences, business travel, and hotel stays plummet during the pandemic.

Nonetheless, organizations must realistically assess where their money is best spent as well as where their peoples' time is best used. As an experienced business traveler myself, I can honestly admit that there is some charm in business travel – some of the coolest places I've ever been were experienced on business trips. On the other hand, business travel is time away from family, it is usually unproductive time, and it is very expensive. Remote and distributed models enable organizations to choose when a business trip is necessary versus routine, and channel that investment into business travel that could yield critical results.

In the remote distributed model, one very essential business trip that everyone in the organization must make periodically is the regular gathering of the organization to build relationships, collaborate, and plan, and generally build that common esprit de corps that forges the organization's identity when they are in full remote and distributed mode, the norm. Investing in business travel for these reasons is critical. Curtailing business travel due to health concerns in the short-term and to the realize the benefits of remote engagement inside and outside the company for the long-term helps make funds available to invest in these critical, culture-building all-hands gatherings.

Summary

We've looked at how remote distributed teams enable organizations to recruit and hire the people that are best suited for the needed roles, regardless of their physical location. We've discussed how this enables not only the acquisition of the best talent but also enables and fosters diversity of the workforce by opening up the geographic span of your recruiting and making it easier for people to interview. We've discussed the shift in thinking about real estate and space, and how a remote organization decreases its need for physical space and may enable the organization to reduce real estate costs in various ways. We've examined the planning and thinking necessary to support these decisions and how the human factors must be considered in planning, organization, and in evolving organizational cultures.

In the next chapter, we will discuss how a permanent pivot to remote/distributed models will both enable and require changes in leadership models, the definition of work, and the evolving integration of work into daily life and routines.

CHAPTER 3

What Will Change

What Will Grow

One of the biggest changes that has happened and will continue to evolve in remote and distributed work environments is a change in styles and approaches to leadership and how leaders see themselves and their teams.

> **Note** The days of defining work as a place you go and productivity as seeing "butts in seats" are dead. The 1970s called… it wants its management style back (it should have sent a text instead…).

Leadership Will Change – Must Change

Pay attention: If you are the type of "leader" (quotes are intentional) who must see "your people" to feel confident that their work is getting done or believe that seeing "butts in seats" is somehow a measure of productivity or commitment, I have some important and serious advice for you – *retire or quit*. It is time to step down, step away or step aside. This type of leadership style is outmoded in nearly all work environments (with the grudging exception,

© Shawn Belling 2021
S. Belling, *Remotely Possible*, https://doi.org/10.1007/978-1-4842-7008-0_3

perhaps, of scenarios where physical presence and command and control management is a necessity) and will not work at all in a remote/distributed work scenario.

Over my career spanning 30 years I've consistently learned about myself and about other people, and I have evolved my own leadership style to that of a collaborative servant-leader. I trust people – I assume that they want to do their jobs well and I expect people to be professional. Until I have cause to believe otherwise, or unless the trust is broken, I lead that way – I assume positive intentions, and manage the exceptions. This approach has served me well as a leader of remote distributed teams – it had to. The success of the business and the successful delivery of the projects and products I was responsible for relied on accomplishing things through people and teams spread across the United States and, in some cases, the globe.

In 2020, as the Covid-19 pandemic forced organizations across the globe to experiment (many for the first time) with remote distributed work and teams, the focus on the practice of leadership in remote work situations intensified. What kind of leadership styles are most successful in remote scenarios? In addition to my own experience and the various examples I share throughout this book, additional research and contemporary articles brought additional insight to this important topic. *(FYI: There is scholarly research available on leadership styles in degrees of remote and virtual settings. For example, the article cited in the following paragraph draws from a study published in the Journal of Business and Psychology in June 2020, found here:* https://link.springer.com/article/10.1007/s10869-020-09698-0. *This study's literature review cites dozens of articles addressing everything from emergent leadership in self-managed virtual teams to expertise and collaboration in geographically disbursed organizations).*

Throughout 2020 and into 2021, I've read dozens of articles and blog posts and been in numerous discussions about leading in remote, distributed, asynchronous scenarios. As a result, I have confirmed that there are a lot of viewpoints on remote leadership. One of the more interesting articles that I reviewed discussed which leadership approach is deemed best suited to successful remote team leadership. Writing in September 2020, Arianne Cohen discussed some research and anecdotes which concluded that the traits that make for a successful in-person leader don't always make for a successful leader of remote distributed teams. Stop reading for a moment and think about your own vision of a leader, or the "traditional" image of a leader: extraverted, confident-looking, seemingly a "smartest person in the room" type – what I often call a "front of the room" personality.

Cohen's article noted that the "front of the room" style does not translate effectively to remote team leadership. Instead, the successful leader of virtual remote teams is the doer – the person who leads by being a reliable organizer, by being accountable for their work and ensuring that others stay on schedule, complete their work, and get help when needed. On remote teams, charisma, personal charm and style count for little compared to real results. It is the ability to do things, to get things done and help others do so, that translates into effective leadership (Cohen, 2020).

Cohen references a *Journal of Business and Psychology* study that tracked over 200 US teams with varying compositions of on-site, virtual, and hybrid teams. The study found that while the on-site teams tended to gravitate toward the "front of room" leader, the emerging remote team leaders were the aforementioned doers who delivered results.

Cohen notes:

> Those chosen as remote leaders were doers, who tended towards planning, connecting teammates with help and resources, keeping an eye on upcoming tasks, and most importantly, getting things done. These leaders were goal-focused, productive, dependable and helpful. In other words, virtually, the emphasis shifts from saying to doing.

Cohen's article goes on to affirm many elements of some points that I make and theories which I advance throughout this book. This confirmation is timely, as post-2020 and post-Covid, the growth of organizations who will continue or expand their use of remote or hybrid teams means that these organizations must understand and foster the type of leadership that is most effective in this setting. Part of the leadership equation along with the formation of successful teams in the remote virtual environment is the ability to trust and to foster trust. Later in the book, I spend more time on trust and the concept of "swift trust" and how this develops on new virtual teams.

Key takeaway Leadership styles and thinking must change to enable and support success in remote distributed work scenarios.

The key takeaway here – leadership styles must change to support and be successful in the world of remote distributed teams. Leadership stereotypes and paradigms will shift as more experience and data proves out the leadership styles that are truly effective. Assess how this will manifest in your organization. Choose to be part of this change. This will require organizational changes inclusive of the culture as well as specialized and directed training for leaders that focuses on the leadership skills and styles that are most effective for leading remote distributed teams.

You Can't Herd Electric Sheep

In late 2019, before the Covid-19 pandemic was even a thing, my leadership team and I were working out some guidelines for remote work options. I was already steering my leadership team and my department in this direction for a variety of reasons, not the least of which was my previous experience with remote work and belief that it was a capability that could benefit our department. One of the directors on my leadership team noted that she had certain people with whom she did not feel comfortable allowing to work remotely – she felt that she could not trust these team members to complete assigned work if not closely observed by her or a team leader. I stopped the discussion to point out that this was not a remote work issue. In these situations, you have a different problem entirely – you hired someone you cannot trust – regardless of the work scenario.

Note Don't hire anyone you wouldn't feel as confident about working on the other side of the country as the other side of the office. Proximity should not equate to productivity.

Remember this: No matter what your work scenario – on-site, remote, distributed, hybrid, whatever – don't hire anyone that you do not feel comfortable with their work approach regardless of whether they are sitting outside your office or sitting across the country. If you have people on your team or in your organization whom you feel won't be productive in a remote/distributed scenario, you already have a people problem or a hiring problem – fix that first. It is also very important to develop a hiring profile that ensures you recruit and hire people who are likely to be successful in remote and virtual settings, and then, once hired, immediately trust them to be conscientious and productive. Whether remote or on-site, my personal recruiting mantras is "hire for attitude and aptitude – assume best intentions, manage exceptions."

Butts in Seats Don't Equal Productivity

I've previously spoken of examples from my time at CloudCraze. When we moved into our new, post-acquisition high-tech office overlooking Wacker Drive in downtown Chicago, the new CEO had deliberately placed his office at the back of the large open office space so that he could look out across the room, see people at the rows of open desks, and feel confident that the work was happening. He could see and hear the outbound sales team making calls and see their "scoreboard," and he could see other members of various teams setting at the long rows of open desk space, "crushing code," talking to customers, and having meetings in the big glass-walled conference room. It wasn't long before it became very clear that he had a real issue with the entire software development team, which was not sitting there in Chicago – nearly all of them were remote and distributed across the country.

It turned out that this CEO's perception (unlike the founding CEO) was that people who worked in the downtown Chicago office were hard-working and productive because they came in by nine in the morning and were there, physically present, until roughly five o'clock in the afternoon. By contrast, the remote software development teams worked a similar number of hours spanning a wider range of start and stop times and were just as productive if not more so – but the CEO couldn't see them working – there was no scoreboard he cared to access to monitor checked in code (we used Jira and typical Scrum artifacts), so he didn't really buy into that fact. The software team often started working around six in the morning and were active into the late night hours, but without a tangible physical office presence of butts in seats right there on Wacker Drive, the CEO couldn't believe in their productivity.

This disconnect between the work that was really happening and the CEO's perception led to a toxic scenario where I was asked to lead the software teams in the same way that the sales people in the organization were being led and measured. In order to foster accountability and competitiveness within a relatively young and inexperienced sales team who were "smiling and dialing", sales management had put up a kind of scoreboard where everyone in the open office could see who was making the most calls and setting up the most meetings. Because the CEO could see the sales people and their scoreboard during the nine to five timeframe, his perception was that the sales team was hard-working and accountable. **Note:** This is **not** how you lead modern software development teams, whether remote or on-site.

I was asked to put similar visible metrics in place for the software team. We used agile practices and worked in sprints, so we were already tracking team velocity for each sprint as a natural part of the overall agile framework we had used for years. All of this information was readily available in our tools and was shared at the end of each "sprint" of development work during release cycles. However, the CEO insisted that the virtual teams make the results of the development sprints public to the rest of the organization and turn it into a competitive situation. This is generally toxic in software or product development, and the complete antithesis of how leaders should use these metrics in agile software delivery.

This approach, aside from being counter to my own beliefs and leadership style, was also confusing to the software development teams and, within a short time, caused their morale to plunge. The moral of this story: Assuming that you hire competent and professional people and have an organizational culture that fosters and requires accountability, creating false competition and using "big brother" metrics can be counterproductive to successful remote virtual teams and organizations. Worse, creating a spoken or unspoken assumption that the "butts in seats" teams are more highly valued and assumed to be automatically more productive than the remote teams is a recipe for failure.

A *Harvard Business Review* article featured the following that sums up the concept that physical presence does not equate to nor should be confused with productivity:

> it will be essential to avoid conflating face time and actual output when assessing performance—so that people don't feel they need to show up to convince the boss that they're working hard. And when in the office, they shouldn't feel obligated to be in meetings or on their computers all the time. If coming back in means only individual work and task-focused meetings, the positive lessons from the pandemic will have been lost, and the organization's performance and culture may be jeopardized (Fayard, et al., 2021).

Remote Is Not a Perk – It's Table Stakes

Some organizations have long thought about remote work as a perquisite, as a benefit, something that can be offered or earned as an option based on performance, or as a retention item – a way to keep someone who might be considering a change. That attitude and approach is no longer a thing – in the organizations of the 2020s, remote work is a normal and expected option, a routine organizational capability. In short, remote work options are table stakes for the post-pandemic workplace.

This takes us back to the leadership and culture discussion. In years past, some organizations and managers treated remote work as something they could use to reward certain people, or as a privilege extended to certain trusted staff who could prove they needed the option and could justify the need, and who had through previous performance somehow demonstrated that they could be "trusted" to be productive remote workers. At one organization where I worked in the mid-2000s, working from home was a benefit, but was assumed to be available to meet an occasional need (meeting the repair person, expecting a delivery, etc.) versus a regular or ongoing situation. There were loose but clear guidelines around the circumstances (example: working from home is not to be a replacement for child care), and as far as I know, it was seldom if ever abused.

Now: Imagine having the following conversation in an interview with a prospective employee in the 2020s (probably via videoconferencing): *The old-school manager:* "Once you've been here a few years and proven yourself, we may allow you to work remotely some of the time. Meanwhile, plan to uproot yourself to work here and have your butt at your desk forty-plus hours a week until we trust you." *The candidate, thinking that they are in a 1990s time-warp:* "Thanks, bye."

My flippancy to make a point aside – in the 2020s and forward, successful organizations will treat remote work and distributed teams as assumed, as an advantage that enables the best people they can possibly hire to work where and when they are most productive. Successful leaders will evolve and build work practices and cultures that leverage remote distributed scenarios to be successful and continuously improve the outcomes of their teams and organizations.

Speaking of Productivity…

I'm a morning person. I love to wake up early, make coffee, and get to work at my desk in my home office. Given a day where I am setting my own schedule versus facing a day full of meetings, I love to be heads-down for three to four hours, then I need mid-morning exercise followed by a meal and a break. I'll muddle through early afternoon administrative work, then I find I get really creative again and jam between 4 and 6 p.m. That's just me. We all have different rhythms of productivity.

At CloudCraze, I led remote distributed teams of software developers whose peak hours generally occurred between 5 a.m. and 9 a.m. and then from 7 p.m. to midnight or even later. As I learned the rhythms of the various people and teams, my leadership approach evolved to become comfortable with the people and teams working the hours that suited their productivity as well as aligned with their other responsibilities, such as their families.

It is important to the example and the point that I want to make that these teams could be counted on to deliver a critical software release, bug fix, or ensure that a client's ecommerce site went live as planned. Productivity was not determined wholly by *when* one worked, and certainly not *where* one worked, but *how* one worked and how that coordinated with the schedules and rhythms of others on the teams.

The pervasive adoption of remote distributed work and organizations both requires and enables a redefinition of productivity. The conversation, in many cases, has shifted and will continue to shift to **what** gets done and becomes a lot less about **where** or **when**, on a day-to-day basis, work gets done. Most people have times of the day when they are hyper-productive and other times where they need a mental or physical break, or both (*I'll talk about combining the mental and physical break to foster creativity later in the book*).

Chapter 3 | What Will Change

In a 2020 *New York Times* article by David Gelles, Automattic founder and CEO Matt Mullenweg talked about accountability for results versus the hours spent at the keyboard:

> For most roles at Automattic, what you're accountable for is a result. You could work 60 hours and not do a lot, or you could work 20 hours and do a ton. It's really about result. And I do believe beyond a certain point, there is a diminishing marginal return to work. I also believe below a certain point, you're probably not going to be able to keep up with people who are working something around like a 40-hour week. But in the middle of the bell curve, there's a lot of flexibility.

… and Flexibility…

Adapting to a world of remote distributed organizations and teams, all of them working at times when they are most productive and working around work and family schedules, means that flexibility is also an expectation as well as a critical organizational competency. Long before the pandemic of 2020, plenty of organizations were experimenting with flexible schedules of varying types to meet worker needs for work–life balance in their careers and lives.

As I described earlier, we were doing this throughout the 2010s at CloudCraze with our software development teams. Automattic's examples throughout this book and dating all the way back to the birth of that company in 2005 demonstrate this type of forward thinking. The difference is that pre-2020, these organizations and examples were often the exceptions – the subject of the occasional article in a business or tech publication, treated like mavericks or visionaries. In the 2020s and beyond, flexibility of working schedules, just like remote work itself, are now table stakes. The organizations and leaders who will be successful in this era are those who not only embrace and support flexibility but learn to lead and deliver successfully with this flexibility.

Inc.com's Jessica Stillman, writing in 2020, examined various aspects of workplace and schedule flexibility. Scenarios such as hybrid in-office/remote work schedules, a "3-2-2 workweek" (not defined specifically by a Saturday–Sunday weekend), and the overall option to build work schedules that work for people's lives define the organization and work model of the 2020s. Employees who got used to this flexibility during the pandemic of 2020 will demand this going forward, and organizations interested in retention, productivity, and reputational excellence will provide it. Another benefit of this scenario is that commuting (whether by car, rail, or other) and wasted time sitting in traffic jams become non-factors (Stillman, 2020).

> **Note** Caregivers should not have to choose between caring and working. Asynchronous remote working models enable both.

Further to the flexibility point – working people with children or other family obligations have long juggled work/life commitments so that jobs duties and life duties could be met. When one or more of the caregivers in the household are working remotely, this both offers and requires flexibility. Enabling one person to focus on non-work needs while the other puts in two to four hours, then switch off so the other person gets in some worktime is one model of flexibility that remote work has long enabled. The 2020 pandemic basically made this a mandatory experiment for many people and many organizations.

It is important to note that the 2020 pandemic saw a disproportionate number of women leave the workforce. This is widely attributed to scenarios where many organizations who went to remote work still expected their employees to largely work during traditional business hours, which is also when other people in their households needed care or assistance with remote school. Unable to do both things, many women opted to stop working. This is grossly unfair and a huge waste of talent. Asynchronous work models enable caregivers to structure their work around the needs of others in their households without being put in the position of choosing one or the other.

I'm concerned that some data shows the possibility of the world going in the wrong direction on this critical issue, and the unfettered embrace of remote distributed work can help fight this. *Harvard Business Review* research published in January 2021 predicts that the gender gap in comparable wages could be exacerbated as some companies and employees return to the office. The reasoning behind this is the antithesis of why and how remote work should function.

HBR believes that when employers offer the choice to work from the office or home or some other location, more men than women may opt to work in the office and more women may opt to work from home. *HBR* quotes a survey from Gartner indicating that managers favor in-office workers and are likely to give in-office staff higher compensation. Connected to the assumption that more of these workers would be men, there's your expanding gender-wage differential. HBR's data shows a different picture of productivity, however – Remote workers show up with a 5% greater likelihood of higher performance compared to their full-time in-office counterparts (Kropp, 2021).

In the 2020s, this type of flexibility is one more example of the expected table stakes that organizations must offer and master in order to win the competition for distributed talent and to be successful in their marketplaces. It is up to the modern organization and leader to make flexible, remote distributed work a reality that benefits people and organizations. Expect to see more job descriptions that include the following: "We'd love to see you in the office at least two days a week – more is fine." Be one of the leaders who makes this happen.

What Constitutes Work Anyway?

During my early-morning walks and runs, I think and come up with reasonably decent solutions to problems and generate new ideas along a particular stretch of a road that runs south out of central Madison and through the suburb where I live. It takes me about 20 minutes of walking (or ten minutes of running) to hit this stretch, and on some mornings, that's when the ideas and solutions come to me. I've had more "aha" moments than I can remember along this stretch of road and am grateful for the hand-held supercomputer that is always with me, enabling me to capture these ideas, solutions or important notes about my work. So – am I exercising or am I working? Or is work and life merging into just living and being?

Dating back to 2012, I've had a habit of mixing exercise and conference calls. It started with the Thursday morning EDL staff meeting. I knew the only time I would need to talk a lot was when I gave the ecommerce team resource and staffing report, so the rest of the time I jammed on my elliptical machine or exercise bike – I slowed down, caught my breath and had my reports open on my iPad prior to it being my turn to report. I kept that habit up until 2015 when the new owners changed the staff meeting to Monday afternoons, with on-premise participation in Chicago preferred and necessary to earn style points with the new CEO.

The Walking Conference Call

During 2020, I resumed the habit of mixing exercise with conferences calls along with another habit that I had refined during my EDL and CloudCraze days: The walking conference call. Depending on one's role, you (like me) may find that you are involved in a lot of conference calls where your presence is somewhere between useful and mandatory, but your speaking parts are limited. You must listen and stay engaged in the flow of the discussion and add your insight or report at appropriate moments, but the rest of the time you are on mute.

The walking conference call is perfect for this. I've found the added benefit of being away from a screen and focusing solely on the discussion helps to sharpen my attention and helps me contribute in a (hopefully) more valuable way. I point these out as two examples of work/life activities that are possible and common in remote work settings. The blending of various activities many would consider "non-work" with "work" activities enables one to maintain important routines like exercise while engaging and even heightening their participation in work activities that do not always require screen time.

When you (or a member of your team) decide to take a 30-minute walk outside your home office to clear your head while considering a work problem – are you working? What about the exercise/conference call examples I offered – are you working? You damn sure are. These and other examples of non-typical work situations have been tried and adopted and are part of the remote and virtual landscape of working in the 2020s. As a leader in a remote distributed organization, it is important for you to socialize and foster the idea that these types of work/life mash-ups are good and okay – they contribute to creative, productive, and healthy people, teams, and organizations.

Something You Do – Not Somewhere You Go

Most if not all of this book assumes that the reader and the organization are primarily made up of what we often call "knowledge workers." Assuming the availability of necessary technology – basically a computer and a broadband Internet connection – the assumption is the knowledge worker can perform their work literally anywhere. The writer, the artist, the independent software developer, and many other thinking and creative types have had the flexibility to perform work wherever it suited them for decades. For these workers, work has always been something they did, and not a place that they went.

For organizations who have built or who will cultivate remote working models and distributed virtual teams, the concept of work being something you do and not somewhere you go is core to the culture that must be evolved or newly created. As I noted earlier, it must also be core to the leadership style that will be adopted by the most successful leaders and organizations.

For many, the 2020 pandemic was their first experience with work as something that did not require a commute to a specialized physical location. This of course was jarring and very challenging for people whose personal space was not conducive to this situation. However, this also enabled people to recognize that "work" did not require the commute and the necessity of congregating in a physical space in order to successfully work or collaborate.

One remote work model that had its "breakout moment" during 2020 is telemedicine. The routine medical office visit that seems at least 50% gathering or affirming information that should already be in the electronic medical record (EMR) system is, for many, a frustrating experience that requires planning much of one's morning or afternoon around it. The move to remote work included aspects of medical practice including virtual office visits and virtual consults from pharmacists, just to name a few.

Expect virtual and telemedicine to continue and improve in the 2020s as both medical providers and patients explore, realize, and then expect, the efficiencies associated with telehealth and virtual office visits. The expansion of virtual care and telemedicine has opened up many options for patients and providers and, in some cases, removed barriers that sometimes prevented patients from seeking treatments. It has also enabled various models for more efficient pharmacies and virtual senior care (Shapiro, 2021).

Other verticals with business model and service similarities will look at the telehealth model and recognize how virtual services can save time and space for themselves and for their customers. Efficient service delivery can save everyone time, reduce operating costs, and further contribute to the flexible work–life balance afforded by remote distributed organizations and working models.

Note Bill Gates used to sleep under his desk and count cars in the parking lot. Now he espouses the benefits of remote work.

Bill Gates was famous during the early Microsoft years for working to exhaustion and then sleeping under his desk. As Microsoft grew, Gates was also famous as a manager who checked to see whose cars were in the parking lot as a measure of their commitment and productivity. In August 2020, I watched an interview with Gates – his attitude had clearly shifted. Gates discussed the concept of work as something you do versus someplace you go from the context of office space savings, relieving pressure on inner cities, reduction of expensive and polluting business travel, and overall lower costs and time savings for businesses, organizations, and people.

Gates noted the innovations in the various tools that enable remote work and offered a prediction of ten years of innovation compressed into a two-year timeframe. The number of enhancements and improvements to video-conferencing tools within the space of ten months of 2020 alone is proof that this trend is likely to continue. Remote workers and organizations of all kinds as well as their customers will benefit from these improvements and demand that they continue.

Gates called out the important benefits to women and families that can be realized in the remote work model, but also noted how important it is to seek balance. Gates observed that remote work models with parents and caretakers both at home facilitates the emergence of, and in fact really requires, complementary parenting skills while also assessing and balancing the importance of all caregiver's work. The Bill Gates of the 2020s has clearly evolved from the Bill Gates of the 1990s (Gates, 2020).

Summary

In this chapter we've talked about the changes that were realized as a result of a massive global experiment with remote and virtual work in teams. We've talked about critical and necessary changes in leadership styles and described those approaches that will be effective for remote leadership. We've discussed necessary changes to assumptions and culture, moving away from assessment of productivity based on visual observation and instead to one based on accomplishment and output.

We've discussed the definition of work and the crossover of work with other activities as beneficial, necessary, and productive in remote scenarios. We discussed flexibility, work–life balance, and the concept of work as an activity that can be performed independent of physical spaces.

In the next chapter, we will focus more closely on leadership in remote and virtual teams and organizations. We will talk specifically about hiring practices focused on trust. We will discuss how to build relationships within remote teams and in remote organizations, and the importance of the onboarding process as well as strong cultures in remote organizations and virtual teams.

CHAPTER 4

Leading Virtual/ Remote Teams and Organizations

Remote and virtual scenarios are the last place that micro-management has any chance of working. In these scenarios, absence of trust is nothing short of destructive. In this chapter we'll discuss key elements of organizational leadership in the contexts of remote and virtual scenarios.

> **Note** Leadership styles, personal traits, building culture, onboarding, and establishing trust are all crucial and all happen somewhat differently in remote scenarios.

Hiring for Trust

When I took over as the ecommerce practice manager for EDL Consulting in late 2012, my departing boss (Rob) walked me through the working styles and personality quirks of each of the members of the team I would soon be leading. I had worked with all of them as a project manager, and had traveled with and met most of them, but I'd now be leading them as their functional manager, and Rob wanted to give me deeper insight into their work styles, strengths, and weaknesses.

We spent the most time talking about John. Rob described John as a "rock star coder" but also as someone whose work habits were not consistent or predictable. That turned out to be an understatement. Over the next three years, I learned that while I could generally trust John's code and architectural decisions, I could not trust him to show up to calls or meetings on time or sometimes at all. In our all-remote/virtual environment, this was a huge problem. This problem became more pronounced as we grew and handled multiple client implementations concurrently, and so the "where's John?" game became less and less tolerable despite his technical ability. It was ultimately the core reason that his promotion to the most senior level of architect was delayed for two years.

I didn't hire John – I inherited him and was responsible for his delivery and growth for three years. We spent most of that time working on his consistency, reliability, and punctuality. The fact that I was willing to invest this time and occasionally cover for his absence while tap dancing in front of clients is testament to his technical prowess. In the EDL remote culture, my experience with John has ever since reinforced my thinking on hiring for trust in remote/virtual scenarios.

Note "Rock stars" are called such for a reason. They can often wow the customer with amazing solo performances, but they also sometimes wreck hotel rooms, say inappropriate things, and puke on the people in the front row. In any culture, but especially a remote distributed organization, be wary of the "rock star" and the impact on the culture.

Trust Is Critical

A manager might be tempted to hire or retain someone they don't fully trust but feel like other capabilities outweigh this issue as long as they can "keep an eye on them." This is a bad decision regardless of the work environment. As I noted in a previous chapter – don't hire someone you don't trust to work effectively across the room or across the country. Build interview scenarios and create expectations that test for and expect the presence of trusting relationships.

Prior to 2020, hiring for remote/virtual scenarios would include discussion of the remote work scenario and a candidate's experience in this setting. Reference checks might include a question on the candidate's performance as a remote worker or as part of a virtual team. Post-2020, the likelihood that a candidate and the hiring manager both have experience in remote work and virtual team settings is exponentially higher, but the conversation and expectation-setting is still critical.

The key qualities you are looking for are accountability and evidence of the classic "motivated self-starter." These qualities are critical for anyone in any job. Within certain assumptions, no one should have to be told to start, to learn, to find ways to deliver value. Questions about a candidate's approach to their first 30 days on the job can help determine if you are talking to someone who will be proactive and own their learning and onboarding. Interview questions that delve into a candidate's sense of self-discipline and how they approach tasks when they have minimal direction and structure can also help provide a sense of how the candidate approaches work.

Hiring Examples

In *The Year Without Pants* Scott Berkun described the hiring ethic at Automattic as a quest to hire "self-sufficient, passionate people." Berkun affirmed what any hiring manager knows – these people are not easy to find. This is one reason for the hiring process evolved by Automattic that includes assigning candidates who make it through the second interview to a contractor gig to see how they perform "live" in the Automattic culture and environment. This is not a speedy process, but it does allow both Automattic and candidates to ensure that Automattic's remote/distributed model and culture and the candidate are compatible (Artiss, 2019).

Collage.com enhanced their hiring processes as the company grew and as they learned from hiring missteps. Managers think through the expectations of a new role or new hire, and the job descriptions and associated interview questions are built around them. Interview questions include discussion of past experience in remote work scenarios. Advancing candidates tackle a real-life situation in a time-boxed setting to determine whether they can address their own impediments and offer solutions versus seek direction (Stanton and Ghosh, 2016).

You may or may not find it feasible to give prospective candidates a sample project or contract test-drive as part of your hiring process, but it is critical to find a path to assessing a candidate's experience and likely success in your remote scenario. Often, organizations and hiring managers feel pressure to fill a role lest the work go undone or the candidate take another position in a competitive job market. A former CEO had a phrase that sticks with me when considering this: *Hire slow, fire fast.* Parsed out, he was essentially saying to take the time necessary to ensure a good fit, and to act swiftly if despite this, it becomes clear that a new hire is not a good fit.

Note Consider and develop ways to assess candidates and their ability to function in your particular remote environment and culture – build in the time necessary to do this well.

Joining EDL Consulting and their all-remote/distributed organizational model in early 2012 was both exciting and a little scary. Once hired, I spent three days at the office in Deerfield getting my laptop set up and going through the usual onboarding/HR stuff, covering key things I needed to know to function remotely (which cloud apps and storage tools were used for what things was, and is, critical).

Without a specific project or client assignment right out of the gate, I had a lot of unstructured time in the first few weeks in which I needed to learn our product, clients, and the Salesforce platform. The sense of accountability I felt in those early weeks has defined my approach to remote work ever since. I felt trusted, and I wanted to show myself worthy of that trust by being ready to contribute as soon as possible.

I don't remember all of the questions I was asked in the interview process that helped the EDL leadership team determine that I was a good fit for the remote/virtual model, but there was one that really stood out to me and that I highly recommend for any interview process. Craig, one of the VPs, asked me about past projects I had led. When I responded with descriptions of the outcomes, he stopped me, acknowledged what I had shared, and said *"yes, but what did you learn?"*.

Note Discussion of how a person handles mistakes and how they approach learning can give you important insight into a candidate's attitude and workstyle.

Hiring for trust includes getting a sense of how a person approaches mistakes and learning: Do they own their learning? Do they acknowledge past mistakes and demonstrate what they learned and how they grew in the process? Do they talk about how issues surfaced and how they responded to them? Look for people who describe collaborative approaches, who describe getting their team involved early and coming up with possible solutions, and a sense of urgency appropriate to the situation. Equally important during this conversation is conveying how your organization approaches learning and mistakes – let's assume that mistakes are handled proportionately and, most critically, as learning experiences, and not as "fault-finding." More later on building trust in your culture and relationships.

In my experience, human resources and hiring managers interests do not always align during the interview process. In short – HR wants to ensure that they get candidates and then ensure a consistent hiring process that won't get the organization sued. The hiring manager wants to get the best possible candidate and wants to learn as much about the candidate and their likelihood of success in the role as possible. I personally struggle with interview processes that require an interview panel ask each candidate identical questions – I prefer, and learn more from, open-ended conversations. In the "identical questions required" scenario, most allow for follow-up questions – this is where candidate-specific follow-ups can facilitate those conversations where one learns about a candidate's experience and approach to remote/virtual scenarios.

Building Relationships

One of the most challenging parts of remote work and distributed organizations is relationship-building. I recall at two of my new roles (both in-person-type jobs) in the early 2000's, I was assigned "lunch buddies" for the first week. Not at all a unique practice then or now, this helps new people meet colleagues and to immerse them in the new culture. This is not the easiest thing to replicate in fully remote organizations. As we'll discuss later, many organizations have on-site or hybrid experiences, and these can support and facilitate the in-person introductions and experiences to build relationships which extend and grow when in full or mostly remote modes.

Regardless of remote or in-person, the most important factor in building relationships is creating opportunities for people to interact and experience one another as coworkers and as humans. This is not new information, but it is critical to reinforce. During 2020, I learned as an experienced remote leader that this was something we needed to cultivate across our entire organization. Although a remote and distributed model may be the way your organization wants to go, this may not be ideal for everyone with regard to forming relationships. The savvy leader recognizes this and intentionally creates scenarios where individuals in small groups and teams have the opportunity to talk about things other than work and learn about each other.

Different people have different comfort levels with this experience, especially in remote settings. Talking about one's hobbies or family over video conference might feel completely different than doing so over coffee or lunch. This is where the leader puts one's self out there, so to speak, to model and show that it is safe. Especially if this is not a comfort zone for you as a leader, it is critical for you to practice and ensure you convey the safety to others.

One of my examples started as a twice-daily emergency response video call as we took Madison College into full remote mode in the spring of 2020. Once it seemed things were in place and going well, we scaled the call (which involved three of my directors and me) back to Tuesdays and Thursdays. As the weeks went by, we found that this twice-weekly call not only helped us coordinate key elements of our infrastructure and support operations, but it also helped us learn more about each other as people, which strengthened our now fully remote relationship in ways that had not emerged while we were working in-person.

Empathy

A theme and quality that emerges from this approach is empathy. *Empathy* – the ability to understand and share the feelings of another person, is critical to the relationship-building that is in turn vital to successful remote distributed environments. Empathy does not come naturally nor equally to everyone – I speak from experience. For a variety of reasons, I found that I needed to learn and practice intentional empathy throughout my career and growth as a leader. The broader my span of responsibility, the more I found empathy as a critical skill set to cultivate as the type of leader I wanted to be. Especially with remote people and teams, listening and learning about the people to learn about who they are and what experiences shaped them helps to frame the relationships that further foster trust and ultimately lead to success in remote and distributed organizations and teams.

Bill Loumpouridis, founder of EDL Consulting, described the critical role that empathy played in developing relationships. Bill put himself in the shoes of the remote team member and ensured that as a leader, nothing he or the in-person team did would create "FOMO" – Fear of Missing Out. Bill felt it vital to relationship-building and to the evolving culture that remote team members felt the same experience and as close to the action as people in the office. Another vital element to relationship and culture at EDL was the open-door policy. Remote team members had a standing invitation to travel and come into the office at any time to work and connect (personal conversation, December 22, 2020).

Contact

One-to-one (1:1) meetings with people are vital to establishing and maintaining relationships. As a leader, regular 1:1s provide opportunities to talk business but, equally as important (especially in remote scenarios) create an ongoing narrative in which you get a sense of who a person is and how they are doing. It's important to establish the type of connection and familiarity that helps a leader determine when someone may need help with their workload, a people or technical issue, or something that is affecting them as a person.

In my time at EDL and CloudCraze, 1:1s were mostly about our work, but over time, helped (along with periodic in-person meetings) establish a sense of each person on my team. This also helped me understand the home office environment each of my remote team members worked in. Often, the people with young kids at home structured their work around the hours when kids and partners needed their attention. Others occasionally worked in temporary office space, and John (discussed at the start of this chapter) shared stories about converting his garage into a man-cave/office.

Establishing Remote Norms and Culture

If you are founding a new organization, you can be intentional about the culture you create that supports remote and distributed work and teams. This was the case for Bill Loumpouridis at EDL Consulting.

Bill built EDL on the concept of hiring the best people, wherever they lived. The national (and ultimately, international) client base supported this approach. In building the EDL culture, Bill always kept the experiences and feelings of the remote people in mind, ensured that as a leader he and the leadership team never did anything that would exclude remote people, and created several practices that kept remote people in the loop at all times. Bill recognized that it was important to ensure one culture for EDL as opposed to a "Chicago/local" versus "remote staff" culture.

Monthly and Annual Meetings

Two important EDL practices, the monthly all-hands meeting and the annual meeting, were critical to EDL's culture.

The monthly all-hands was much like any other tech firm's all-hands, but it was structured in a way intended to engage and recognize remote staff at all times. If remote people happened to be at the Deerfield office for the all-hands, they'd typically get a shout-out. Many of the presentations were done by remote staff working from their homes or at client sites around the country. Gratitude for everyone's work was always part of the closing.

The annual meeting was something special. The annual meeting was a mix of company business and planning along with families-included celebration. Employees were encouraged to bring their families – all expenses paid. By recognizing that their families were an important part of each employee's humanity, EDL enabled each employee to know each other better at that level. For me as a leader, the chance to meet spouses and children and remember them as part of the being of each member of my team was critical to forming relationships. These practices along with the standing invitation to travel and come into the office at any time to work and connect were essential to the EDL culture and helped foster a successful distributed organization.

Also key to the culture Bill wanted was strong human resources leadership. Bill emphasized how critical this leadership was to build and reinforce the culture at EDL. My first contacts were with the vice-president of human resources, Sue. From our earliest conversations, EDL's remote work culture and practices were prominent parts of the interview discussions, and Sue's role in cultivating the culture was critical. It is a testament to the effectiveness of this approach that eight years after my hiring and onboarding, I accurately remembered most of these details for this writing prior to confirming them (personal conversation, December 22, 2020).

Culture-Building Examples

The EDL narrative outlines approaches to remote culture-building similar to those taken by the founders of Automattic and Collage.com (and doubtless innumerable other remote/distributed organizations). At Automattic, founder Matt Mullenweg (once beyond the early, product-focused inception of WordPress) found that an organic series of decisions created the foundation of a distributed and merit-based culture.

One key culture decision was to focus on the core product development and creative engine of the company while ensuring that the supporting and ancillary functions did not constrain growth (*It is worth noting the contrast with the EDL story – EDL involved HR as critical to development and reinforcement of the culture, while Automattic saw HR as potentially distractive to the core function of the organization. Neither is "right"; rather, this reflects differing philosophies – both were successful.*)

The original, volunteer and open source-based foundations of WordPress created the ability and expectation to add contributors from wherever they happened to be located – the original cohort of employees were based across the United States and Europe and expanded to a global presence. Automattic uses a mix of remote and in-person meetings throughout the calendar year to foster relationships and maintain culture and cohesion (Berkun, 2013).

Value Accountability and Problem-Solving

Developing or evolving a culture is partly about being clear on what is valued. A core assumption of successful remote and distributed scenarios is that the outcomes, the value creation, is what is important – as opposed to being in your home office chair and on-camera for a specific time. Automattic's merit-based approach is an example of this type of culture. "Automatticians" are accountable for what they deliver as opposed to how many hours they work (Gelles, 2020).

At Collage.com, founders Joe Golder and Kevin Borders evolved a culture that intentionally enabled talented people to work from their homes – wherever they were. As Collage.com grew, leaders were groomed and promoted from within while Collage.com recruited new talent interested in remote work and capable of successful collaboration and problem-solving while part of a distributed team. As the Collage.com culture evolved, founders and early leaders placed particular emphasis on collaboration for problem-solving. Similar to previous examples, Collage.com uses twice-annual in-person meetings to foster relationships and the culture of collaboration (Stanton and Ghosh, 2017).

We Already Have a Culture… Now What?

The clear themes that emerge from these three examples is the importance of intentionally considering and developing culture from the organization's early days. For existing organizations moving to remote and distributed scenarios, the culture discussion takes a different meaning. How do you adapt remote within an existing culture? How does culture adapt to remote work?

With people and organizations around the world having gained experience with remote work and tasted the potential benefits of this model, the genie is out of the bottle, as it were. There are doubtless organizations that will feel remote work models don't work for them, and cultures that will resist any permanent move to this model.

Leaders Must Lead

Adapting starts with leadership. Leaders must understand the organizational culture and assess how potentially long-established cultural norms may work for or against successful remote work scenarios. In Chapter 3 we discussed the need for leaders with outmoded thinking about people and leadership to move out of the way. If an organization's most senior leaders are ready to move to remote and distributed scenarios, it is there – as with any organizational change – that the sustained support for this change must start.

There are plenty of bromides, old saws, whatever, about culture – how it eats strategy for breakfast, how it can be an obstacle to change, etc.… The shift to remote work is different. Why? Unique to this change is the fact that nearly every organization capable of doing so had to experiment with remote work and distributed teams whether their cultures were supportive or not. With the Covid-19 pandemic's forced experiment, plenty of organizations were forced to overcome cultural obstacles to remote work and learned a lot in the process. These experiences provide hurdles to cultural impediments that might not have otherwise surfaced without harder organizational change work.

Apply Learnings from the Experiment

As with a new organization, leaders in established organizations must be intentional about this change. It's critical to take the learnings that most organizations gained during the Covid-19 pandemic and assess what worked well and what elements did not work as well This information will serve as a blueprint for long-term adoption of remote distributed scenarios. Key to this learning and assessment is how the organization's culture affected and was changed by experience with remote and distributed work and teams.

In large organizations, it is likely that some functions were able to be fully remote while others found it necessary to operate in partial remote modes, and of course some functions had to be maintained as primarily on-site work. Assessing how each functional area adapted and worked with other areas will help leaders determine how to make positive outcomes as permanent cultural change and how to adjust expectations and norms in those areas that may benefit from or be interested in long-term remote, but whose initial experiences were not as positive.

Evolving a culture from on-site to remote requires consideration of how you will gather as a remote or hybrid organization, and what the focus of these gatherings will be. Will you be doing regular all-hands meetings with all-remote or a mix of on-site and remote people? What time will you be doing these? If you are making this transition, think about how you want this to work. Know your people and teams – do they appreciate social time and activities via video conference, or do the majority of people find these trite and poor use of time?

Note Not every organization and culture will value emphasis on sharing personal details and family news in video conferences. Proceed accordingly.

A family member of mine shared a negative experience that reinforces the importance of knowing your audience: Periodic video conference meetings of busy medical professionals with time-sensitive workloads were considered "must-attend" and required each participant to come up with family photos or a short description of their latest family plans for each meeting – a waste of time for busy people who preferred to focus on updates and critical information and then get back to their work. While well-intentioned, the meeting organizer did not empathize with the needs of the participants.

As of this writing, my team and I are working this out. When I took the CIO role at Madison College, one of the things I did immediately was to establish monthly all-hands meetings as a time to connect, celebrate accomplishments, and share news. When we went remote, we continued this practice and tried to inject fun and social opportunities into the all-hands. This had mixed success, but helped us learn and tune the remote meetings.

Example – Some people appreciated the 4 p.m. start and 5 p.m. transition into a virtual happy hour, but I also got feedback that this was problematic for some as this infringed on the daily transition into family time and some felt they could not participate without making a choice between family and connecting with coworkers.

Example Practices

EDL and CloudCraze, where I spent 2012–2017, built their products and services on the Salesforce platform. A pioneer in cloud computing and Software-as-a-Service (SaaS), Salesforce was and is a leader in building a great workplace culture, and routinely wins recognition as a great place to work. Adapting and transitioning their culture to a fully remote status required them to consider ways to leverage their infrastructure and existing practices to ensure they remained a great place to work. Some of the things that Salesforce did during this transition serve as excellent practices to evolve an on-site culture to a remote and distributed culture. We did similar things at Madison College throughout 2020 and will continue to enhance these practices as we implement remote work as a permanent capability:

- Make communications as transparent and people-centric as possible
- Ensure employee benefits adapt to meet the needs of remote employees
- Ensure that technology evolves and adapts to support remote employees
- Design opportunities to connect as people with lives and interests beyond work

Whether or not you are a multinational SaaS leader like Salesforce, practices like these can help transition your culture and practices to support successful remote and distributed work scenarios (Unikel, 2020).

Communications

This is the most critical element of culture transition to get right. When an organization transitions from a mostly on-site model to a remote and distributed model, those opting or taking the opportunity to work remote may feel like they are away from the center of action and communication. Therefore, it is critical that organizational change and culture adaptation prioritize efficient and transparent communication.

Remote virtual technology makes communication relatively cheap from a literal and figurative perspective. What I mean by that is it is not expensive in terms of effort or people's time to quickly share information that you think others might be interested in. Tools like Slack, Teams, and similar enable a continuous and democratic sharing of information across the organization. If you have a nugget of information or a solution to a coworker's impediment, you can share it without writing an email or calling a meeting. It just goes in the communication stream.

An example of this practice is one that we evolved at CloudCraze. After years of using Skype for instant messaging, some members of my development team started using Slack. We liked it so much that it became the default communication tool for the development and support teams and ultimately the whole technical side of the company. The downside of this was that sales, marketing, and other support functions felt left out of this constant communication stream. We had to teach them how to engage in this steady flow of communication without interrupting their flow or ours.

The ability to create teams and channels for specific functions, groups, interests and similar within tools such as Slack and Teams is a truly amazing and productive capability. Rather than rely on email or scheduling meetings at specific times in order to communicate and collaborate, the remote worker can simply subscribe to various channels and teams or be assigned to the appropriate channels and have immediate access to a steady flow of communication and information. In these scenarios, no one should feel cut off or left out unless there are failures of set up or inclusion

The Continuous Asynchronous Virtual Meeting

That header is a mouthful, but it describes a practice that my leadership team and I put into practice. We used to have a Friday stand-up meeting where we did what I called "check out of the week." When we went all-remote, I evolved this to a continuous chat in our Microsoft Teams channel. Rather than schedule a meeting, we developed the habit of typing updates from our various perspectives in the channel all morning, so that by mid-day my leadership team had a good picture of how the week had gone, anything important happening over the weekend, and a sense of what they should be thinking about for the week ahead.

Benefits

Depending on the scope and history of your organization, it may be that you are already dealing with benefits in multiple states or even multiple countries. On the other hand, if your organization was local or regional, the move to remote may introduce the necessity to determine how you tailor benefits to serve the needs of remote and distributed workers. Payroll and benefits consultants can help organizations deal with nationally and globally distributed workforces. My college used one of these services when we adopted the policy that our faculty and staff could live and work in any state that had the appropriate state tax relationship with Wisconsin. Using an expert helped our human resources and finance teams considerably when we made this important policy change.

Technology

As a CIO, technology that supports a remote and distributed workforce is near and dear to me. The concept of the digital workplace, a common experience that is easily accessible for everyone regardless of where they are located, is critical to successful remote and distributed scenarios. A culture change may involve the relationship between people, technology, and how IT enables and supports a remote and distributed organization.

IT's own culture and strategy must shift to support remote and distributed scenarios. At EDL, everything I needed to do my work was cloud-based, with the exception of the office productivity suite. Storage, collaboration tools, and of course our product platform (Salesforce) were all cloud-based. During the Covid-19 pandemic, those organizations that were most successful at pivoting to remote scenarios were those that already had robust systems in the cloud and a good employee digital experience that was ready to go. These systems and experiences are necessities for the remote distributed organization.

At Madison College we had already made strides to provide a secure remote desktop and VPN experience – this served us well, and our Covid-19 experience enabled us to adjust our strategy to accommodate a future where more of the college's faculty and staff (as well as students) would work remotely at least some of the time.

Connections

Where communication is the most critical element to get right, connections that enable a remote and distributed workforce to know and experience each other as people beyond work is the most difficult to achieve. I think it is difficult because every organization and culture has its own balance and expectations around these types of connections.

If your culture already valued people in a primarily on-site scenario, your culture will and should continue to value people in forging and maintaining connections as you transition to remote. On the other hand, if your organizational culture tended to separate work and nonwork, it will feel non-authentic and contrived to attempt to change the culture as you transition to remote and distributed work.

Onboarding in Remote Organizations

Onboarding in remote and distributed scenarios is even more crucial than on-site onboarding. The remote employee, new to the organization, may have taken the position partly due to the opportunity to work remotely. But it is still a transition to a new organization, and it is critical that the onboarding experience be one that enables the new person to get up and running efficiently while also creating intentional opportunities to convey and immerse the new person in the organizational culture. Despite what should be every effort to provide information and quick help resources, a new employee who encounters an impediment during remote onboarding can't go to the person in the next desk or cubicle for help.

The nature of the organization determines the priority of onboarding knowledge. For example, I've been adjunct faculty for several universities, and the onboarding process prioritized access to and knowledge of the systems that supported teaching, with HR systems and routine IT knowledge a close second. At EDL and CloudCraze, learning Salesforce (since it was the platform on which core products and services were based) was a key component of onboarding along with coaching for those new to consulting.

Digital and Paperless

The transition from an in-person to a remote model should be accompanied by careful re-examination of business systems and onboarding. Anything that is not already paperless and highly automated must be made so during this transition. Nothing could be more frustrating than attempting a fully remote onboarding process while still dealing with paper-based elements and inefficient business processes. A link to a cloud-based HR system accompanied by a secure authentication method should enable the remote worker to establish their identity/user account, complete mandatory start-of-employment tasks, and simultaneously enable access to email, productivity tools, and further technology set-up and resources.

Ensuring new remote staff can find the tools needed for work quickly and efficiently is critical. Assuming the availability of technology devices appropriate to the role, delivering an optimized digital workspace should be a paramount objective in the transition to remote and distributed scenarios. Note that cloud platforms are key and are more efficient than VPN access or virtual desktops into on-prem systems. Prioritize immediate access to tools such as Slack or Teams. Make sure that new remote employees have access to any channel that provides a new person instant connections to team members who can help them as well as access to communication streams that start the immersion in vernacular, TLAs (Three-Letter Acronyms), and similar elements that make up the organization's practices and culture.

Gear and Swag

Nothing says "welcome – you are one of us and we are glad you are on the team" like swag: apparel, coffee mugs, pens, notepads, laptop cover stickers and so forth. Whether on-site or remote, providing welcome swag (see Figure 4-1) to new staff helps to foster the belonging that in turn helps new relationships develop. Consider this as part of the onboarding process if you aren't already doing this.

Figure 4-1. Samples of onboarding "swag" for a new remote employee

Another "welcome" element to consider for the new remote person is a home office stipend. Plenty of organizations built from Day 1 as remote distributed companies do this. During the Covid-19 pandemic, many organizations chose to provide equipment or funds to workers suddenly faced with setting up a home office. As discussed in Chapter 2 and upcoming in Chapter 6, ensuring that everyone can build a good experience in their home office is critical to culture and productivity. It is also worth a reminder that this stipend is a cheaper expenditure than furnishing a desk, cubicle, or office in a commercial building. One of the coolest things that EDL and CloudCraze (pre-2015) did for new employees was give them their choice of a PC or Mac laptop. Remember John? He and another team member were allowed to contribute their own money to enhance the laptop stipend in order to buy high-powered gaming laptops. Did these machines get used for non-work gaming? Sure. Did they contribute to morale and also provide high-powered work tools? Hell, yes.

Experiment and Iterate – Ask the People

The main objective of onboarding at any organization regardless of on-site or remote is to enable the new person to start adding value as soon as possible. There must be some allowance for the level at which a new person joins the organization – if they are in an entry-level role, naturally the assumption of prior experience is much lower than if you are adding somebody with significant experience in that role or to a more senior or leadership role.

I joined EDL Consulting in January of 2012, and as noted earlier, spent the first couple of months onboarding. Because I did not have a specific client assignment in my first few months, EDL also had me look at elements of their practices such as project management and organizational knowledge management – two key elements of the onboarding experience.

After six months at EDL, I provided a write-up of what I had learned during the onboarding experience with specific suggestions for improving onboarding, all in the service of ensuring that new people could add value as rapidly as possible. What follows is an abstraction of the specific examples to apply broadly to any organization that is leveraging knowledge or technology-oriented people to deliver their products and services:

> **Standardize repeatable processes** – anything your organization does or will do repeatedly should be standardized so that there is one common way everyone does that thing. For example, if you are a project-oriented organization, project management practices such as estimating and writing project statements of work should be standardized.
>
> **Develop curriculum** for your specialized business systems, products and services. If there are platforms that will be critical for new people to learn, make sure that the first weeks on the job immerse them in new platforms or tools and include training and certifications where appropriate.

Convey critical examples of "how things are done." For example, if there are certain ways that certain customers, departments, or colleagues are typically handled, make sure that this is conveyed early in onboarding.

Make sure there is a feedback loop so that new people can share their progress, ask questions, and, most critically, share what is working and what is not working so that the onboarding process can be continuously improved.

Examples

With countless remote organizations to serve as examples, it is easy to research and find resources on which to model potential onboarding experiences and best practices. I encourage you to do so after reading this book – there is more to learn than I could possibly capture here. That said, following are some examples from organizations that have been remote-native since their inception and provide good examples of successful best practices.

Automattic

As a remote-native organization, Automattic has the remote onboarding thing down. It starts with the Automattic approach to having candidates test-drive the work and the culture as part of the interview process. Before even joining, candidates and Automattic know if there is a cultural fit, and new people have some sense of how they will interact with colleagues and access resources and information. At Automattic's WordPress, all new people spend the first few weeks working in WordPress's version of customer support, called "Happiness." This ensures that everyone understands the customer experience, regardless of their role (Berkun, 2013).

Collage.com

Collage.com initially onboarded new people by giving them progressively larger and cross-functional projects, until their growth caused some issues with this approach. Collage.com adapted their onboarding approach and provides new people with information pertinent to their roles as well as start-up meetings with senior leaders and colleagues in their area, followed by paired work with a more experienced team member. Monthly and post-project reviews help ensure new people are onboarding effectively (Stanton and Ghosh, 2017).

Basecamp

Basecamp makes several products but is best known for the project management software product that became its namesake – Basecamp (they were once called 37signals). Basecamp is another remote-native organization that has had lots of time and practice developing remote onboarding practices. Basecamp assumes that the average onboarding period is about three months and assigns a "buddy" to new hires to ensure the new person has a designated person to help them get up to speed. This buddy, along with an Ops buddy and the new hire's assigned manager collaborate to support the new hire. Basecamp also "eats its own dogfood" – it uses its own product as part of the onboarding process (Basecamp, 2020).

Summary

This chapter has covered a lot of territory – all from the perspective of what leaders need to do to ensure the creation or evolution of culture and practices that will foster a strong remote and distributed working environment. We've discussed hiring practices, relationship building, development of practices and culture, and the criticality of the onboarding process, especially in remote and distributed scenarios.

The next chapter will focus on people. As part of this focus, we will discuss trust in more detail and how trust is built in remote teams and organizations. We will discuss specific personality types and how they respond and adapt to remote and distributed work settings. We'll also discuss various approaches and theories on motivation and how they work in remote scenarios. Finally, we will talk about approaches organizations can use to combine on-site and in-person time with remote and distributed work to build trust, reinforce culture, and ensure the best possible combination of on-site and distributed work practices and cultures.

CHAPTER 5

Psychology of Remote Teams

Trust, People, and Connections

Trust is a most valuable currency within any organization, and in remote and distributed organizations, where coworkers and team members do not regularly interact face-to-face and may be geographically separated most or all of the time, it is crucial to success. In Chapter 4 we discussed the importance of hiring for trust. Now, we're going to focus on how to build trust in remote scenarios. Going forward, everything I'll cover assumes that you have hired with two-way trust in mind and are committed to developing and maintaining a culture of trust and accountability within your remote distributed organization.

© Shawn Belling 2021
S. Belling, *Remotely Possible*, https://doi.org/10.1007/978-1-4842-7008-0_5

Trust

Trust, along with its close partner Accountability, is the most basic currency in any organization. The confidence that exists when one person says, "I'll take care of that thing" and others know that the thing will be taken care of is what enables any working relationship or team, on-site or distributed, to function. Trust is also the currency that enables people to have open and honest conversations and share enough of themselves so that others develop understanding of what makes them tick, and openly admit to mistakes and actively seek to address them and learn from them.

Trust is something that typically takes time to develop between people and groups. It is also extremely difficult to regain when lost or damaged. Leaders build trust by describing and embodying the type of positive environment they will foster, protecting teams, and following through on commitments. Leaders build trust by creating environments where mistakes aren't punished – they are corrected and learned from.

People create trust through accountability and delivering on commitments. When a team shares a goal and everyone on the team does their part to meet the commitment, the team builds trust in each other. This trust in turn enables the team to extend their effort, knowing from experience that everyone on the team will do their best. When a coworker makes a mistake and turns to another for help and gets that help without criticism or judgment, trust is developed. When leaders hold themselves accountable and create an environment where accountability is expected and valued, trust grows.

In on-site scenarios, the factors that facilitate and create trust are supported by proximity and opportunities for social interactions that help build familiarity and knowing others. In remote environments, trust evolves in different and important ways. There are fewer non-work social opportunities, and so trust and accountability tend to be developed through delivery of work and follow-through on work and project-related commitments.

I've taught a master's degree course on managing project teams for about 12 years. The original course and one of the texts we use was developed by my mentor, Dr. Ginger Levin. Dr. Levin and her writing partner, Parviz Rad, identified the obstacles to building trust on virtual teams in their 2003 book *Achieving Project Management Success Using Virtual Teams*. Their book sourced research going back to the mid-1990s regarding the challenges associated with building trust on virtual teams – this is not a new topic.

Rad and Levin describe trust as the key ingredient necessary in preventing the physical and structural separation between team members from manifesting as psychological distance. Rad and Levin further note that online interactions can preclude the multi-channel cues that make up full communications, resulting in lower-bandwidth scenarios for developing understandings of personalities and capabilities. Trust is listed as one of the key people attributes necessary for virtual project organizations to ascend to higher levels of maturity and competency. At the highest levels of maturity and competency, virtual team members share concerns, work approaches, and engage in collaborative leadership based on trust (Rad and Levin, 2003).

Collage.com – Examples for All of Us

Kevin Borders, co-founder of Collage.com, references the importance of trust as critical in remote environments. Borders notes that trust in remote scenarios starts with leaders and creating what he calls a "mistake-friendly culture." When leaders admit mistakes and share challenges they are facing, it models for the whole organization. Borders describes how retrospectives help to create trust, and how the assumption of positive intent by all team members is critical. Leaders must be accountable and own those retrospective findings that could prevent future problems.

The importance of personal connections is a key part of the Collage.com approach to trust. By intentionally creating practices that encourage discussion of personal and family details and reinforcing these practices, managers stay connected to and develop empathy for their teams while people in different functional areas learn about their coworkers. Seeing others as people and not just coworkers is an important factor in building trust.

Reinforcement of shared objectives helps remote teams avoid or resolve disagreements – Borders notes that in remote environments people may engage less often, making the shared goal critical to enabling people to trust one another's decisions. I have found this to be an important component of team meetings and all-hands meetings. I use these meetings as opportunities to reinforce our ongoing and consistent values and to remind groups and departments of the consistent "north stars" that we are striving to evolve and achieve.

Like many other all-remote organizations, the in-person all-hands is an important part of how Collage.com builds and maintains trust. These periodic in-person opportunities have proven essential to Collage.com, as they have for Automattic and countless other organizations. In addition to in-person leadership Q&A sessions and cross-department collaborations sessions, the after-hours social opportunities that occur at gatherings such as these are incredibly valuable to fostering and cementing relationships and trust that last long after the in-person gatherings are done (Borders, 2020).

Swift Trust

Have you ever joined a team of people you'd never met before to work on a task or a project, and found that you all gelled and began to get things done relatively quickly and with a minimum of concern as to who was in charge at the moment? One name for that experience is "swift trust." This is the unspoken agreement that a group of like-minded and competent people quickly develop that enables them to assume the best of one another and focus on accomplishing work versus jockeying for leadership or worrying about who is doing the most or least work.

Swift trust can be more challenging to develop on virtual teams and in remote settings, but it can be achieved, and it is critical for success in these scenarios. Leveraging the initial atmosphere of assumed positive intentions, shared commitment, and benefit from the outcomes helps to foster swift trust and also helps to create experience on which to build more lasting forms of trust through the experiences described earlier.

Keith Ferrazzi shares two key points for leaders that help with creating swift trust: Communicate the abilities of the team members, and ensure the team has clear goals. Ferrazzi further describes the importance of creating empathy, leveraging regular and quality communications, and shared power and leadership based on the stage of the project as additional elements to leveraging swift trust and developing sustained trust on virtual teams (Ferrazzi, 2012).

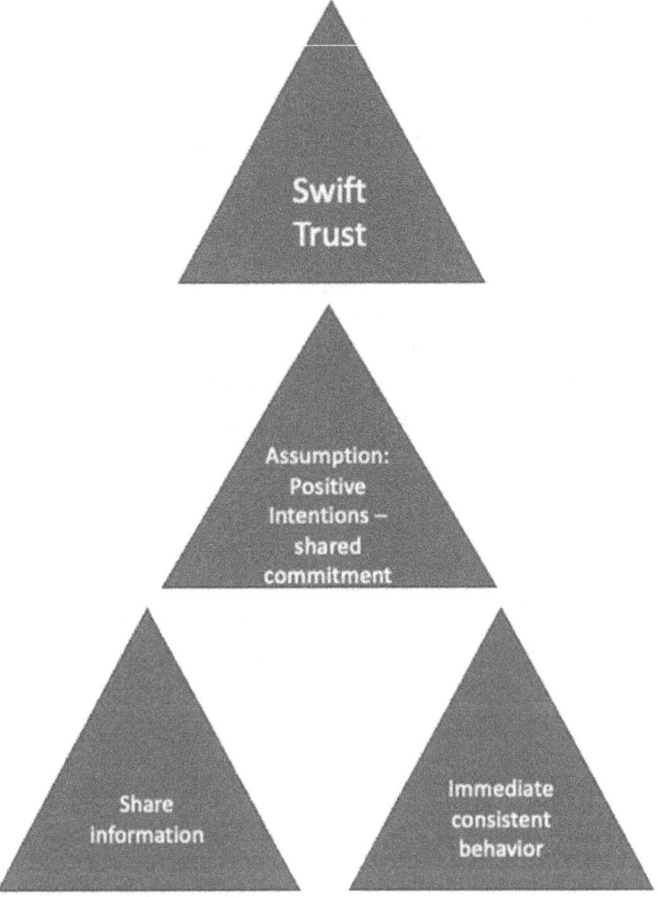

Figure 5-1. Foundations and components of Swift Trust

Personality Types – How They Adapt

People approach and respond to remote work scenarios in different ways. No one who's spent any time researching or working with the topic of people and personality types recommends slotting people into groups and generalizing their behaviors and tendencies. Yet, understanding these general frameworks and having conversations with the people in your organization to better understand their needs and responses to workplace configurations is a key element to establishing a successful remote and distributed organizational model.

Organizations operating in remote and distributed modes prior to 2020 already understood the importance of acknowledging and adapting to people's personal styles and needs and had various methods for doing this in place.

Plenty of other organizations learned this for the first time during the Covid-19 pandemic. Organizations forced to move to a remote work model had an opportunity to learn how people responded to this scenario and to develop methods to support them and the varying needs that people with differing personality types and life situations have when working remote.

As I noted – it is not a great idea to put people into groups and generalize their behavior – but in order to efficiently structure and facilitate some of the points I want to make, for the next few paragraphs I am going to do just that. Of the many models for gathering data and preferences from people and grouping them based on these data and preferences, one of the simplest is the grouping of introverts and extroverts. The oversimplified explanation of the two groups is as follows:

> **Introverts** like to process and think – they tend to gather information, including information from interactions with others, and then seek some time and solitude to process and come up with ideas and solutions. Introverts often prefer to work alone for periods of time and find this to be productive. Most critically, introverts find that engaging with groups of people for long periods of time drains them of mental and physical energy, and after such engagements need time to recharge.
>
> **Extroverts** like to talk through their ideas and form new thoughts and solutions through these interactions. The lively exchange of ideas helps form and improve their thinking, and the engagement with groups of people in these types of sessions energizes them. Extroverts desire interaction with others to maintain that energy level and engagement.

Despite some stereotypes and popular culture around the supposed benefits that forced isolation and remote work has for introverts, there is not a style that is good, bad, better, or worse for remote and distributed scenarios. What is critical is to learn about people – whether new hires or current staff – and ensure complete understanding of how they will adapt and thrive in a remote distributed environment. My personal experience as a leader in remote distributed settings prior to 2020 and during the Covid-19 pandemic helped to form some broad conclusions:

> **Extroverts** may find the remote/virtual team experience generally unsatisfying – leaders must find ways to compensate. This could include frequent one-to-one check-ins, regular engagement in chat channels, engagement in small groups of others with similar needs, and activities such as book clubs and special interest groups.
>
> **Introverts** may find the remote/virtual experience generally satisfying but could become disengaged – leaders must be alert to this and find ways to compensate. Given the many competing priorities that leaders face, it can be too easy to leave the introverted worker to their own devices, assuming that, based on what you know, he or she is okay with this.

It is useful to consider the variations in learning styles that become even more important in remote and distributed environments. With a totally on-premise workforce, it is easy to gather groups of employees together for training and learning. The employee learning and organizational development departments of organizations often rely on this type of training, combined with various types of online learning, in order to convey mandatory information or for training on things like soft skills.

In a remote distributed environment, there are multiple ways to convey similar information that can account for variations in personality types and learning styles. Extroverts who appreciate learning from a speaker or presenter can benefit from a live webinar. Others who may prefer not to be present in the live webinar can watch the recordings. Everyone can take part in asynchronous online learning through various learning systems.

As a professor with over 20 years of working with adult learners in executive and graduate programs, I believe that professionals are responsible for identifying their learning needs and objectives and making these needs known to their instructors or employers, while also being accountable for ensuring their learning needs and objectives are met. Remote and distributed organizations can offer a variety of ways for the adult learner and worker to get their learning needs and objectives met.

In summary – people with different personalities approach and respond to remote work scenarios in different ways, with extroverts potentially finding it an unsatisfactory experience and introverts being totally happy with it. The key is for leaders to recognize these qualities in people and teams and find ways to adjust. Recognize that the extroverts may be craving a chance to be in the office whereas the introverts are perfectly happy with extended periods of no on-site/in-person time, but run the risk of becoming disengaged. Learning and organizational development efforts must also account for personality types and learning styles, and the remote distributed organization benefits from a variety of ways to approach this.

Motivation – Theory and Practice

In a course that I teach on leading project teams, we spend an entire unit on motivation. It's an important topic and a key leadership skill to have and to foster in any work environment, and in remote and distributed scenarios it is critically important. As with personality types, there are a myriad of theories and approaches to motivation, and one could devote an entire book to them – but not here. For the purposes of this section, I'll nod to Maslow's Hierarchy of Needs but spend most time covering some basics of Motivation-Hygiene Theory as well as Theory X and Y management and how these two approaches have applicability in remote and distributed settings.

Maslow's Hierarchy

Many people are aware of Abraham Maslow's Hierarchy of Needs (if you want more than a cursory overview, take some time to research the origin and details of Abraham Maslow's seminal work on what motivates humans). Maslow essentially noted that motivation in humans starts at the level of getting their basic survival needs met, works through levels of safety, love and relationships, and tops out at self-actualization. Safety and self-actualization are the most germane to discussions of workplace motivation. People who feel safe are more likely to trust, collaborate, and speak their true opinions. I wrote a paper and presentation years ago that connected the degree of safety one feels in their job with their ability to speak truth to power in the workplace – this is a real thing. At the top of Maslow's hierarchy, people who have all of their more basic needs met are operating at a level of achieving their best selves and making the most of their personal capabilities through their work (see Figure 5-2).

Chapter 5 | Psychology of Remote Teams

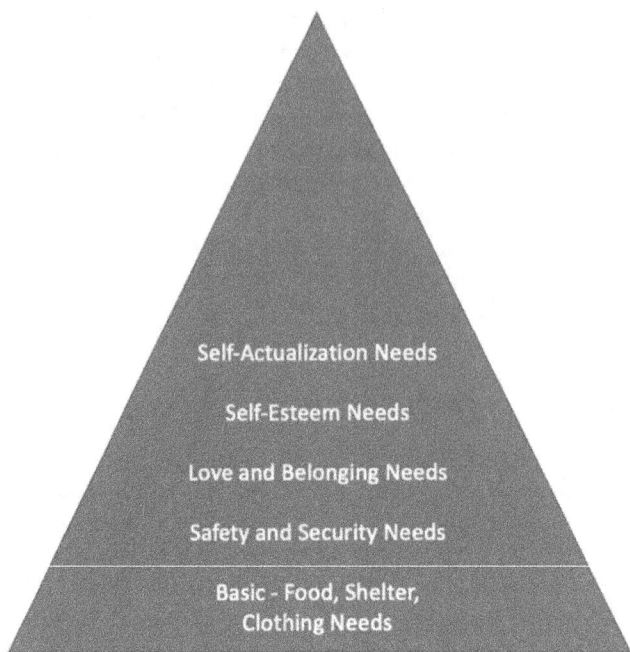

Maslow's Hierarchy of Needs

Figure 5-2. Maslow's Hierarchy of Needs

Motivation-Hygiene Theory

Frederick Herzberg theorized two primary components that contribute to the degree of satisfaction that people experience in their work. "Hygiene" in this context refers to elements that are not necessarily motivators, but can create issues if they are not present or handled effectively – salary, policies, leadership, working conditions, and relationships are prime examples. Motivators are elements that help to create satisfaction such as the work itself, recognition and achievement, and opportunities for responsibility and career progression.

Dissatisfaction with Job	Two-Factor Principles	Satisfaction with Job
Hygiene Factors:	As motivation factors improve, job satisfaction improves.	Motivation Factors:
Working conditions Relations with coworkers Organization work rules and policies Performance of manager and leadership Pay and benefits	As hygiene factors improve, job dissatisfaction decreases.	Achievement Recognition Responsibility The Work Opportunities for Advancement and Personal Growth

Derived from Frederick Herzberg, 1968

Figure 5-3. Herzberg's Motivation-Hygiene Theory (Derived from Abraham Maslow, 1943, 1954)

Motivation-Hygiene theory is important to remote and distributed work scenarios because elements from both categories will influence the creation and evolution of culture and practices and are within the sphere of leaders to tune and improve. Aside from salary, the leadership culture and style, policies and practices and the accommodations and support systems for remote workers are critical hygiene factors to consider in building or evolving a remote distributed environment.

The implication for leaders and organizations is this: Creating remote and distributed work environments that foster trust, that have flexible rules and policies, that facilitate positive relationships with coworkers and assume the presence of accountable and knowledgeable leaders will have as much of an influence on the success of your remote distributed organization as pay and benefits, assuming that these are competitive for your vertical or industry.

EDL Consulting and the culture created by Bill Loumpouridis is a perfect example. As consultants in a specialized field of software development and ecommerce, EDL employees were well-compensated and got their pick of the best possible technology with which to do their jobs. We had reasonably cool swag as well. However, similar boutique consulting firms sometimes offered higher compensation. People who left EDL to work for the competition often found that the culture was not as conducive and supportive of remote work and their career growth as the culture that Bill created at EDL. Not only were the hygiene factors present at EDL, but EDL provided opportunities for achievement, recognition, growth and advancement, and challenging, cutting edge work in our particular field of ecommerce and software as a service on the Salesforce platform.

Theory X and Theory Y

This is one of my personal favorites regarding management and motivation and helps to illustrate the mindset that modern managers must have or learn in order to be effective leaders. Douglas McGregor developed the Theory X and Theory Y approach to describe the mindset of managers and their attitudes toward employees. Put simplistically:

> **Theory X:** These managers generally believe that people don't want to work and therefore need to be managed and motivated through rewards for working and punishments for not working. The classic micromanager fits in the Theory X category, and organizations built around this approach tend to be hierarchical with lots of management layers to provide supervision and hold everyone accountable. This is also the approach of the manager who does not trust people unless they can see them and thinks that butts in seats equals work and accountability.

> **Theory Y:** These managers generally believe that people like work – that work is a natural and productive part of the human condition and therefore people find satisfaction and self-expression in working. Theory Y assumes self-motivation, ownership, and responsibility, and therefore typically a flatter and more collaborative management style is present in these organizations. This approach is a natural fit for the remote distributed environment.

If you are a Theory X leader – ask yourself why this is the case. Seriously consider whether this approach and personal style is valid and effective in a 21st century knowledge and technology-oriented workplace. There are doubtless some fields and areas where reward and punishment and micromanagement are valid leadership approaches, but the scenarios in most remote work settings are not those and the Theory X approach will be destructive.

If your organization tends to Theory X – this is a critical and potentially limiting factor in the successful long-term adoption of remote and distributed models. Consider whether it is possible to transition the dominant leadership approach given the traits and styles of the most senior leaders, and the tenure in office (and possible attrition) of senior and mid-level managers who ascribe to this approach.

Theory Y leadership is in the DNA of most "from Day 1" remote distributed organizations. Founders tend to be highly motivated on their own, and their early hires mirror, by necessity, this approach and attitude. As they grow and scale, remote distributed organizations intentionally recruit and hire for, then foster and reward the Theory Y approach.

As you and your organization evaluate the adoption of remote distributed as a long-term organizational and working model, it is critical to evaluate the extent to which Theory Y leadership is present in your organization. The presence of Theory Y leadership and motivation is a critical factor in the success of this transition.

Overall, the remote distributed, virtual organization or team requires nuanced application of many of these motivation techniques and approaches. Because of cultural differences, it may be necessary to focus on individual motivation, since no single motivational approach would work culturally for the entire team. Similarly, it is important to consider cultural factors in motivation, because in some instances and cultures, rewarding the individual can be counterproductive – we will discuss this in a later chapter.

Motivation for virtual team members must also account for and address the potential feelings of isolation and disconnection some virtual team members may feel, depending on the circumstances. In cases where part of the team is colocated and part is virtual, the virtual team members may feel excluded or less valued due to the physical separation, and benefit from focused efforts to highlight their contributions to the team or project as well as aforementioned and intentional work by leadership to avoid this happening at all. I previously noted some research that supports tendencies by some managers to consider people who come into the office to work as more productive and higher performing than remote workers – be active and intentional in assuring this does not happen as you design and evolve your remote distributed organization.

This same issue may arise based on countries and cultures – if team members from a particular country or culture dominate the make-up or proceedings of the team, other members may feel less valued and require focused efforts to motivate them and show appreciation for their role and work.

Consider – as a leader, traveling to visit virtual team members, or consider conducting a virtual team meeting from various team member locations. This example sends a clear message to each virtual team member and the entire team that they are valued and important wherever they are and can be highly motivating.

Using In-Person Events to Build Connections

One thing I learned during my time leading remote software development teams at CloudCraze was that even though we were from inception a fully remote and distributed team, we needed to gather periodically to plan, brainstorm, and whiteboard, and also to build and grow our personal connections and keep our "esprit de corps" as a team. My experience and the experience of companies like Automattic, Collage.com, and countless others is that connections and team spirit are hard to maintain without the cadence of intentional on-site gatherings. The models for these gatherings share common elements, so I'll give some examples from the CloudCraze on-sites I organized from 2015 to 2017 and add some additional examples from Automattic and Collage.com.

CloudCraze – November 2015

CloudCraze was acquired by a group of Chicago investors in August 2015. As part of the post-acquisition reorganization, I took over as vice-president of software development and support. One of my first moves was to organize an on-site all-hands meeting of the software development and support team that November. It would be the first time that the entire team had ever gathered together, and for many, the first time that they had met each other.

This meeting also coincided with the need to complete and release a version of our product that had been in progress all summer. The work had stalled due to the acquisition and due to the annual fall Salesforce conference in San Francisco, which tended to consume everyone's energy. The gathering would be an opportunity to introduce myself as the new leader as well as introduce the new director of engineering who was promoted to this role as part of the re-org.

We gathered on a Monday, had a huge social outing at one of Chicago's famous pizza joints, and started and renewed relationships over numerous adult beverages. Work sessions focused on structure and expectations of the newly formed unit along with presentations from other leaders. The final full day was consumed with the entire team gathered in a massive conference room testing and fixing final bugs before releasing the new version of the product.

This first meeting set the pattern for subsequent meetings. As we completed each release of the product – spring, summer, and fall – we planned an on-site gathering in Chicago. We started on Monday, with people arriving from all over the country, stopping in the Chicago office, and then attending a large and generally raucous social event that evening. Other leaders and people from other parts of the company often joined for the socializing.

Tuesdays were typically an all-hands discussion of the release we were completing. We brought in other parts of the organization such as professional services and sales and marketing to brief them on technical elements of the new product. We also performed a release retrospective, discussing practices that worked well and good decisions as well as things that did not go as well and decisions we would revisit for future releases.

In some of these meetings, we weaved in question-and-answer sessions with our C-level leadership, training on security and new platform features, and other activities that benefited from having the entire team present in-person.

One to two days were devoted to planning the next release. Reassessing the product road map, finalizing and committing to features, and planning the next month of work consumed the remainder of the on-site. Socializing after hours continued, with groups of people self-forming along with planned activities.

Examples – Automattic and Collage.com

Both of these organizations engage in similar all-hands gatherings a few times each year. Automattic tends to do theirs in different locations, while Collage.com does theirs twice a year in the same spot. Both organizations share the goals of in-person meetings – foster relationships, celebrate accomplishments, have fun as people as well as coworkers, and also accomplish some work-related stuff.

Both Automattic and Collage.com attest to the value of these on-site/in-person gatherings, including the after-hours socializing that occurs, as valuable and important to building relationships and enabling their success during the majority of time that the organizations are in fully remote distributed operations. This reinforces both formal studies and practical notions that you tend to trust and look out for the interests of someone you have met, shared a meal or a beverage with – even better, someone with whom you have created a unique and positive memory with – which further supports the importance of these periodic in-person gatherings.

Adopting the Practice

If you are building or transitioning to a remote and distributed scenario, I highly encourage that you plan for similar practices as those described here. The intentional gathering of an entire team or entire organization at least once and ideally a few times each year is a proven and effective way to build and enhance the relationships that are foundational to trust, productivity, motivation, and overall satisfaction. The time, resources, and money spent doing these and ensuring they are fun and memorable experiences will prove to be valuable investments.

Think about your culture and the overall personality of your organization. There are doubtless elements of your particular organization or line of work that will influence how these on-site gatherings can go. You may have specific work rules or even regulations that determine, for example, whether adult beverages can be part of the equation, and what you can spend and how. Regardless, take the time to think these through and make sure that these in-person gatherings of teams and organizations happen. They build the bonds that enable trust, empathy and effective remote work teams.

The Best of Both Worlds

Remote and distributed scenarios are not an all or nothing proposition. Perspectives that state that all work and organizations will go remote or that state that there is no substitute for in-person work are absolutes and will not be realized. You can have it both ways, and your people can, too. In fact, it is likely that your model for remote and distributed work will include time in the office and time remote each week or each month for most of your team.

Earlier in this chapter, I wrote a bit about introverts, extroverts, and motivation. These elements are unique in each person and influence the degree to which people want or need to be around others as well as work independently. As well, work/life situations will afford opportunities to work from the office on some days, home on others, and the favorite coffee shop or the library on still others.

Assume Hybrid

We like hybrids. Hybrids enable us to have our cake, and eat it, too. Or enjoy two flavors of ice cream at the same time. Or the economy of an electric motor with the power and range of an internal combustion engine. Or cloud-based and on-premise IT systems. You get my point. As you consider models for remote distributed work, your most likely scenario is the hybrid where people spend some time in the office and some time working from somewhere else in any given period of time.

Creating the expectation where a mix of on-site and remote work is the norm is the most realistic and optimal way to go after so many have had the opportunity to experience remote and distributed environments. People will want to have it both ways – they're going to want to spend some time on-site and they're going to want to have the flexibility of remote work. This arrangement provides opportunities for people to determine their own needs for contact and social working – encounters that foster relationships and build trust, which sustain them when they are working remotely and distributed.

As a leader and as an organization, it is critical to foster and enable that flexibility, and build practices and systems that seamlessly support it. As a leader, it is important to consider those work scenarios that would be best served by having people present – and then challenge that. Ask yourself and your team – why? Is the interest in having people gather in-person based on habit or a bias? Or are there practical reasons to do so? The best thing a leader can do is figure out what "hybrid" looks like for their particular situation, articulate a vision, and do your best to make it so.

Four Generations in the Workplace – Differing Expectations

Another thing to keep in mind – we have four generations in the workplace, and there are pretty broad interpretations of what constitutes "work" as well as levels of experience with technology. Older generations may be wedded to the "nine to five" model, while younger generations are already accustomed to different hours and different models of "in the office" versus remote and distributed scenarios. As leaders we need to accommodate and, in some cases, coach others through this.

Potential case in point: You may need to mediate and coach in scenarios where older workers, used to being in the office during set hours and potentially less comfortable with the technology and tools that enable remote meetings and collaboration disagree with a project schedule or collaboration approach proposed by younger team members who are comfortable with remote, flexible scheduling around work/life balance, and the tools and tech that enable this.

It is critical to keep in mind that each generation's perspective has value – no one here is right or wrong. As you build the remote distributed culture of your organization and determine where you need policy, keep in mind the needs and perspectives of each of these cohorts and plan to be flexible and iterative. You will doubtless learn as you gain experience and work through various scenarios.

Summary

This chapter focused on people and various aspects of human behavior, expectations, and motivation in remote and distributed scenarios. We discussed the importance of trust and how it is developed, and we looked at the importance of leadership attitudes and approaches to motivation. We discussed how to leverage on-site gatherings to build and enhance relationships, and how the likely model for most organizations will be a hybrid mix of on-site and remote work, where people spend days in the office and work elsewhere during the week for a variety of reasons and benefits.

In the next chapter we will focus on best practices and tools that ensure remote and distributed organizations operate effectively and create the best possible experience for everyone.

CHAPTER 6

Practices and Tools

Practices and Tools Support People

Let's assume your unbridled success getting the people elements of remote and distributed scenarios right (and you will). Let's also assume the likely case that your organization will opt for a hybrid of remote distributed and on-site environment. The success of your remote and distributed model will depend on the processes, practices, and tools you adopt and evolve.

All practices and tools must share the common goal of assuring and supporting a common and productive experience for everyone, whether on-site or remote. By "common," I mean that everyone has the same *good* experience – *technically and culturally*. By "productive," I mean that being off-site and distributed never in any way creates impediments to getting things done whenever and wherever someone is working (assuming proper tools and Internet access as table stakes).

The Common Experience

Picture this: It's 3 p.m. on a Monday afternoon at a downtown Chicago cloud software company. The *on-site* executive team assembles in a conference room for the weekly operations meeting. The CEO's admin dials up the conference call session while the CEO, CFO, and executive VP exchange inside jokes and chat about each other's families and weekends while teasing the admin about a relationship. Meanwhile, the *remote* VPs of software development, product management, and customer success join the conference call, catch part of the banter, and start wondering what is being discussed and when the meeting is going to get started.

What's wrong with this scenario? Situations like this create an "in-crowd" and an "out-crowd." An environment where the remote members of the team are not part of the pre-meeting banter means the on-site team is not only wasting time, but potentially creating an adversarial or non-inclusive culture. In previous chapters, we discussed the importance of creating an environment where remote people are never any less included than on-site people – intentionally avoiding anything that might alienate remote people and create FOMO: Fear of Missing Out.

This means that meetings, collaboration sessions of any kind, presentations – basically, anything that involves a mix of remote and on-site people and participation – must be optimized to ensure the same experience for remote people and on-site people. This can take various forms. There are some practitioners who recommend the practice that if some members of the team are joining the meeting remotely, everyone does the meeting as if remote – from their offices or desks.

Examples: Everyone joins the meeting using Teams so that everyone has the same experience and can participate similarly in any informal chatter as well as the formal work activities of the meeting. *Similarly* – if large contingents will be joining from various locations via teleconference, have everyone do the call from their desks so that everyone has the same experience and to minimize sidebars and chatter in conference rooms. *Lastly* – if you have a multinational participant group, consider the *timing* of the meeting and ensure it is at either a convenient time for most, or at the least inconvenient time for as many as possible.

Practice Makes Perfect

The last 25 years have given us a wealth of tools and technology to support remote and distributed work. The evolution of telephony, videoconferencing, and various collaboration tools is, when you think of it, mind-blowing. Prior to 2020, existing communication and collaboration tools were constantly and regularly enhancing their capabilities. For example, standalone plug-ins and programs enabled whiteboarding for videoconferencing sessions so that one could whiteboard on a tablet and display it on a different computer to mirror in a video conference session.

During the Covid-19 pandemic, software products such as Zoom and Microsoft Teams added collaboration capabilities rapidly to meet the growing needs of a sudden global remote workforce as well as the needs of students and teachers. Whiteboarding apps emerged and improved, and then whiteboarding was added to some of the videoconferencing tools – things evolved and changed fast. Bill Gates noted that the research and development on these tools was exponential and that we were seeing ten years of innovation on these products compressed into two (Gates, 2020).

I learned long ago that a critical element to successful use of any communication tool, whether a conferencing phone or a newly enhanced video conferencing package, is to practice with the tools and systems prior to using them to support important meetings and presentations. Using these tools and systems well is not something you want people figuring out as they spin up a meeting or presentation involving lots of people. Create expectations within your organizations that new tools will also come with training for users, think through how you will support these tools, and require practice prior to relying on a new tool.

Training Is Essential

As 2020 evolved and organizations began first-time use of tools for video conferencing and collaboration, the need for good training became quite evident. At my college, our help desks were overwhelmed with requests for support on how to use teleconferencing, video conferencing, and similar tools. Students, faculty, and staff all needed training and support to use these tools effectively. Because we were in the process of gradual adoption of these tools when the pandemic hit and we had to pivot immediately to all-remote operations, the training and support practices were not all in place.

Whether you are starting a new organization that will be remote and virtual from Day 1 or transitioning to a hybrid of remote and virtual work, training on the tools themselves as well as best practices for operating effectively in this model are important to developing an effective organization.

Train on Tools

With such a spectrum of communication and collaboration tools available to the modern remote distributed organization, it is critical that organizations plan for and deliver on the training needed for everyone to use these tools effectively. Everyone – from the CEO to the newest administrative support team member – should be basically competent in these tools, and if a position requires regular or constant use of these tools, the people in these roles should be experts.

Depending on your organization, you may or may not have dedicated resources for developing and delivering this training and supporting these tools. Some organizations without a dedicated training or support team choose to identify power users who can assist new people or new users in the effective use of these tools. Whatever your training and support model, there are two good practices to keep in mind:

- Practice with tools prior to using live – don't waste anyone's time.
- Factor in learning curve for new tools, people, cohorts.

Avoid Tool Proliferation and NAFTS

With growing numbers of people gaining experience and expertise with remote communication and collaboration tools, it is natural that these same people also form opinions and attachments to these tools. When new people join an organization, they bring these opinions and attachments in with them. Similarly, more tech-savvy people often become early experimenters with new tools and then advocate their use as part of the organization's approved and supported tool set. My advice – *slow down*. Beware of what I call "Not Another F***ing Tool Syndrome" (NAFTS).

Leaders and tech leaders who are responsible for ensuring tools are supported, secure, and function properly within their organizations need to take a stance and create some hurdles to allowing new tools onboard. Ask the following questions:

- What need are you hoping to address?
- Do we already own a tool that does this or 80% of this?
- Will adding this tool force people to open yet another app or browser tab?
- Is this tool secure, and can we secure it?
- How does this tool use and secure our data?
- What is the license model and cost of ownership?

Previously, I noted that we have four generations in the workplace. This is another driver for NAFTS to manifest. Depending on attitudes and generational expectations, people may expect to use whatever tools they like best. Similarly, when under pressure or in an emergency, people tend to use what they are familiar with and what simply works the way they need it to work. This is not out of an interest to disregard existing tools and practices; it is out of urgency and necessity.

At my college, it happened that we standardized on Microsoft Teams and Cisco WebEx as our videoconferencing tools. There were plenty of people who pushed to use Zoom, but for various reasons we chose not to use or support Zoom, even though Zoom is also a perfectly fine and capable tool, and one which I personally use weekly in my work as a professor. Tool proliferation is expensive – not just due to the software licensing, but from a maintenance, training, and support perspective. Proceed carefully.

Beware of Free

While I was leading software development and support at CloudCraze, the software development team switched from using Skype for instant messaging to Slack shortly after Slack was created. The adoption of this powerful tool was rapid, and we began to use it as the de facto method for communication on the software development and support team. The engineering teams, QA team, and support team all developed norms and expectations for use of Slack. The awesome part about adopting Slack was that it was free – sort of.

It turned out that, at the time, Slack had a 10,000 message archive limit. This became a situation, because one of the benefits was the ability to maintain conversations, snippets of code, and answers to questions in the various Slack channels and threads. My engineering and QA leaders came to me in something of a panic when they realized we were coming close to the 10,000 message threshold and begged me to buy a subscription.

Although I would've preferred more advance notice of this, I was fine with this given that I, too, was an adopter and advocate of Slack. The irony was that as I was about to give approval to spend money on a Slack subscription, Microsoft announced their pilot version of Teams. Since we had a Microsoft subscription that allowed us to trial Teams, there was interest in trying it before committing to Slack – we gathered feedback for a few weeks and then went ahead with Slack.

As a CIO, I have dealt with several variations on the theme of *"we have been piloting this great new tool that does XXXX, and we think it is great, and we want to purchase an enterprise license and make it available to everyone."* This request of course comes after the early adopters have gotten a small cohort of users onboard who now consider the tool essential to their jobs. *In summary – be out in front of this.*

Common Tools – Hardware and Connectivity

I use the phrase "digital ninja" to describe the mindset that everyone in an organization should be equipped to work from anywhere on short notice. That means laptops or powerful tablets with keyboards are the default computing device, and that every employee is provided the appropriate equipment to set up a mobile workstation, whether temporary or permanent.

To maximize efficiency and productivity, make sure that remote workers have good equipment in their home offices. This means dual monitors. Make sure you talk with people about their home work station – make sure that you're educating people and providing resources on ergonomics, on the importance of good broadband service, and talking with people about their home Wi-Fi set-ups. You may consider encouraging people to upgrade or even fund upgrades to slow broadband or outdated Wi-Fi. These capabilities and set-ups are basic table stakes for effective remote and distributed teams.

Common Tools – Software

There are so many good software products available that are designed to enable efficient collaboration for remote distributed organizations. Many of these have been designed by organizations that were also remote distributed from Day 1, so that ethos and experience is baked into their product. This section is not going to dive deep into specific tools, nor advocate for any. One of the common denominators behind adoption and use of these and other tools is to minimize the use of meetings and email as methods for communication.

Web-based portals and team sites offer virtual distributed teams asynchronous collaboration, discussion threads, and document storage and editing capabilities. Capabilities like announcements, issues lists, discussion threads, contact information, document management, task tracking and status reporting, and many other capabilities available through these tools make them a valuable and effective method for virtual team management and communication.

With many platforms, team members can subscribe to pages to receive alerts when information is added or changed. Other capabilities often include the ability to establish workflows so that a task initiated by one team member is automatically passed to the next and on through the workflow until the task is completed.

Following are a few examples of organizations using specific tools to help their remote distributed organizations and teams operate efficiently and effectively.

WordPress – P2 is a WordPress theme used for the internal blogs created for project logs, the name for which rapidly morphed to "P2." P2s became one way that projects and teams in totally remote WordPress announced their existence. P2 usage is considered as about 75% of communication, and so important in the culture that the phrase "P2 or it didn't happen" emerged. This is one example of a company "eating its own dogfood," the nickname given to the practice of using and testing one's own products (Berkun, 2013).

Collage.com – Software company Atlassian makes a popular tool called Jira. At fully remote Collage.com, Jira is used to track code development, bug fixes, tasks, and quality issues. Cross-functional teams can see where a specific issue or piece of work is in process with minimal use of email (Stanton and Ghosh, 2017).

Basecamp – Another totally remote/distributed company, Basecamp sets up instances of their own software for internal activities such as onboarding. Managers set up a Basecamp instance for new employees to track onboarding tasks such as setting up storage, security, repository access, and similar. According to the Basecamp employee handbook, they run their whole company on their own product (Basecamp, 2020).

Madison College IT – Prior to 2020, use of collaborative tools was relatively limited – our web development team were Slack users, and I, along with a few others, were evangelizing for Teams adoption. The Covid-19 pandemic quickly made Teams indispensable as we moved to fully remote operations. As a Microsoft shop, use of cloud-hosted Office 365 tools including SharePoint and OneDrive enabled collaboration on documents, and platforms such as VMWare enabled us to provide secure virtual desktops to an expanding customer base.

CloudCraze – In the early days of my time with CloudCraze, Skype was the de facto instant messaging and telephony tool, and Go2Meeting was used for more formal and organized remote meetings. Dropbox was our storage tool, we used Google G-Suite for intranet and document collaboration and of course Salesforce provided sales and CRM functionality as well as the entire ecosystem on which our product was built. By 2014 we had moved from Skype to Slack for instant messaging and related communications. When we were acquired in 2015, we became a Microsoft shop, using Office 365 and all of the capabilities therein.

These are just a few examples – countless organizations are using tools in various ways, for various functions, to operate fully remote and hybrid remote/on-site organizations.

As with hardware and connectivity, the key is to ensure an efficient and common digital work space – a set of proven and effective digital tools that are securely accessible from anywhere your people will be operating. Organic adoption can go a long way to determining the right tools to use, but beware of tool proliferation.

Communication and Collaboration

As I was writing this manuscript, I was reflecting and wondering why I felt so much busier and stressed throughout 2020 as compared to having equally demanding remote roles and responsibilities from 2012 to 2017.

Chapter 6 | Practices and Tools

Upon reflection, I realized this was because CloudCraze had been a remote distributed organization from its inception. With CloudCraze, I'd have multiple instant messaging threads open with people all the time. We collaborated constantly, both synchronously and asynchronously, while also taking care of work tasks like developing proposals and estimates. Scheduled conference calls happened when needed, but the normal channel and platform for communication was Skype and then Slack. Voice conversations were organic – often the Skype message I'd get from one colleague was "U free?" as a prelude to a voice conversation.

By contrast, most of 2020 involved replicating as much as possible the cadence and structure of what had previously been in-person on-site meetings. As organizations transitioned to fully remote distributed scenarios, much was made of how tools and platforms could be used to replicate the in-person experience. Many leaders, including me, recognized that meetings and face time did not equal productivity, but old habits die hard.

The lesson here as you build or evolve a remote distributed organization is to be very conscious of this and be intentional about the practices you create and evolve. There is no automatic need to create or replicate an "8 to 5 Monday through Friday" workday, unless particular needs of customers or partners make it necessary.

Later in this chapter, I will reference material developed by Matt Mullenweg of Automattic which describes a hierarchy of autonomy in remote distributed organizations. Part of the growth through this hierarchy is less synchronous and real-time and more asynchronous and autonomous work and collaboration, with the ultimate goal being a workplace operation and culture judged solely on producing value and results. More on this later.

Remote Communications and Practices

Organizations that are built from Day 1 as remote distributed organizations will naturally define their norms and culture when it comes to methods and tools for communications. Organizations that are transitioning to remote or hybrids of remote and on-site must be intentional about communication channels and protocols as they evolve.

Note It is important to allow teams to develop their own norms regarding communication and tools. Leaders should step in only when necessary and very judiciously.

Maya Hu-Chan describes some important factors to consider when transitioning from an on-site to a remote environment. Hu-Chan recommends activating your sensitivity to various cues – she calls these "human antenna" –

and being aware of things like pauses in typing, brief silences, body language, and other non-verbal cues as to how people are feeling and engaged.

Hu-Chan notes the importance of knowing your audience and being particularly sensitive to avoidance of insider/outsider dynamics that come from sports references, inside jokes, or use of vernacular that is specific to a language or culture.

I've previously emphasized the importance of assuming best intentions and managing the exceptions. Hu-Chan reinforces this – in remote and virtual communications, assume good intentions, even if the tone or words in an instant message or email initially upsets or confuses you – there is a good chance this is not intentional.

Similarly, Hu-Chan cautions on the use of public channels such as Slack, Teams, or similar for praise or criticism. For example, introverts may be uncomfortable with the attention that public praise brings. Public criticism can be devastating to anyone. Globally, it's important to note that not all people and cultures are comfortable with public praise and certainly not public criticism – "loss of face" is a factor in some Asian cultures. Similarly, people from cultures that value the collective good versus individual achievement may find public individual praise uncomfortable. Even though virtual online communications can be efficient, these are not always the best channels to use for praise or criticism. Consider taking these types of interactions into different, one-to-one communication channels. To do this effectively, it is critical for leaders to know their teams and backgrounds and to treat everyone as individuals (Hu-Chan, 2020).

Cameras On, Cameras Off?

At CloudCraze, I hardly ever turned my camera on in Skype or during Go2Meetings. It just wasn't part of the culture. We saw each other at enough in-person opportunities and built relationships such that we could rely on voice and written communications to convey needed nuances and other elements of communication. In other organizational cultures, "cameras on" has become important, and in some cases become a bone of contention.

The argument in favor of adding video as a communication channel in remote organizations is that the additional element added to voice by seeing facial expressions and potentially body language is important, and helps people understand the overall message more effectively than voice or written words alone. One idea is to recommend camera on when speaking, as a minimum.

It is important to step back and examine the value provided by access to facial expressions and so forth. Are you attempting to replicate what would otherwise be an in-person meeting as exactly as possible? If the situation and people involved call for visual cues as well as audio and written cues, the richness of a video conference may be appropriate. Then, ask if that event itself must happen synchronously. If this is an "inform" type event, the need for synchronicity may not be as important versus making the recording available for consumption when it is convenient for people working varying schedules.

Audio-Only Is Often Fine

I find some of the best thinking and brainstorming with colleagues is when I am walking and I am in audio-only mode, talking through a problem or an idea with a few colleagues. I don't know if it's the walking, or if it is the total concentration on the verbal dialogue that helps me come up with fairly good solutions and outcomes. I think about this often, especially in a culture where we do have reasonable pressure to have our cameras on much of the time.

When you are working with people with whom you have an existing relationship and understand their personalities and communication styles reasonably well, a phone call or audio-only conversation is perfectly fine to accomplish whatever you need to do. Remember, some of us used to conduct quite a lot of business exclusively via telephone and voicemail. In the age of electronic communications where a phone call that is not preceded by an email or text can be considered intrusive or jarring, it is important to be mindful of this. When planning voice communications with people you may not know as well or in different parts of the organization or hierarchy, it is a good idea to reach out via email, text or instant messaging first. You can establish the communication preference for a voice-only or video conference, and then proceed accordingly.

Synchronous and Asynchronous Communications

The various tools and the ceremonies we have built in our organizations in many cases have their roots in an assumption of common working hours, typically 8 or 9 a.m. to 5 or 6 p.m. As I noted earlier, the first five years of remote work experience for me involved a lot of asynchronous communication taking place outside of that typical band. Organizations that are remote and distributed from birth typically leverage a lot of asynchronous communication, because they have *not* built their culture around the typical ceremonies present during a structured eight to five workday.

Organizations transitioning from a traditional on-site workday model must consider how they can free and enable their employees by consciously assessing the typical workday structure with its synchronous ceremonies, and intentionally creating more and more freedom and opportunities for asynchronous collaboration. Without this intentional transition, much of the benefit and efficiency from remote distributed operations will not be realized.

Five Levels of Autonomy

I've made multiple references and examples of Automattic and WordPress, as well as founder Matt Mullenweg's thoughts on remote and distributed work and organizations. Given that Mullenweg and Automattic have over 15 years of experience operating as a remote distributed company, the examples, ideas, and practices that can be considered and adopted from Mullenweg and his organization are extremely valuable and applicable in any discussion of remote and distributed work scenarios.

Mullenweg offers a five-level model for assessing and intentionally developing autonomy in remote and distributed work scenarios. In all of my research prior to this book as well as for this book, Mullenweg's model is the best definition I've come across. The discussion starts with an understanding that there are some jobs that require physical presence: police, firefighters, dentistry, barbers, and more. For the purposes of this discussion, we acknowledge that these types of jobs aren't suited for this model nor are the focus of this book. Mullenweg notes these organizations as Level 0.

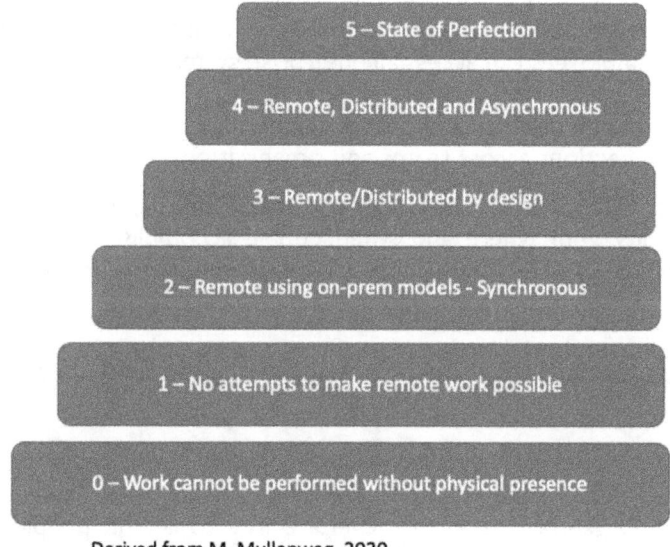

Derived from M. Mullenweg, 2020

Figure 6-1. Automattic founder Matt Mullenweg's Levels of Autonomy

Level One: No intentional work or process to support remote work. In an emergency, the organization could run in a remote model for a few days, but a lot of things would just wait until things were "back to normal." Nothing is optimized for remote or distributed work.

Level Two: The organization essentially recreates the processes and workday structure that they did or do while on-site. Mullenweg notes, and my own experience confirms, that this is how many organizations operated during the initial weeks and months of the Covid-19 pandemic.

This model contributes to the screen time fatigue that many experienced and spoke about as the pandemic moved forward. If you spend big chunks of your on-site workday in meetings, it follows that you would structure your remote and distributed workday replicating similar meetings – this is not the level of productivity or autonomy that is achievable in a remote and distributed environment.

Level Three: At this point of maturity and capability, organizations are intentionally equipping remote workers with gear that supports a good home for remote office experience as well as adopting more asynchronous work practices to replace scheduled synchronous meetings.

Mullenweg notes that the importance of good written communication emerges as crucial at this stage. During synchronous meetings, a document may serve as a central repository for notes and do-outs from real time collaboration.

At this stage, a robust security model is critical to ensure that remote distributed employees can access all enterprise systems securely regardless of where they are located. It is also at this point that the organization should be thinking about intentional and regular gatherings to maintain physical and personal connections across teams and organizations.

Level Four: At this level, more work and operations happen asynchronously. True flexibility with where and when people accomplish work is realized, because the focus is on what gets produced as opposed to when.

This level assumes a very high degree of trust has evolved within the culture and between people and leaders. Organizations at this level have ensured that people have excellent equipment and may have even funded improvements to home offices.

Synchronous meetings happen less frequently, which highlights their importance and the need to ensure they are properly structured and productive. Organizations at this level are free to recruit people from any location and are not bound by geographic limitations or physical proximity. Mullenweg contends that the asynchronous model also leads to better decision making and employee retention.

Level Five: Mullwenweg provides this level as aspirational and likely not fully possible – describing organizations that are so optimized and performant that their performance is beyond any that an in-person organization could. People at these organizations are able to devote equal time to their physical and mental health and are realizing their highest levels of creativity, self-actualization, and best work (Mullenweg, 2020).

Cultural Awareness

Throughout this book I've used phrases like "table stakes" and "blocking and tackling." These are examples of colloquialisms rooted in American sports culture. More examples from my vocabulary include "call an audible" and "game day decision." I say these a lot, but at times, I do everything I can to consciously purge these from my vocabulary. Why?

Depending on the size and scope of your organization, remote distributed work may mean working with people from or based in other countries and with differing cultural experiences. As a leader in a remote/virtual environment, it is critical to model cultural awareness and avoid using vernacular that excludes people who will not understand it. This goes beyond vernacular to recommend an entire curriculum on becoming culturally aware and culturally sensitive. If your organization is or could be a multinational distributed organization, or includes people and customers from multiple countries, this next section is a primer on this topic.

Going Global

Working with people from other countries and cultures is a great opportunity to expand one's knowledge and understanding, and at the same time these differences present challenges to effective communications. The key to success is understanding how various cross-cultural factors influence communications and being proactive in managing these factors.

Cultural norms and differences can lead to challenges in communications. Leaders and members of globally distributed organizations need to be aware of specific cultural norms they may encounter and how they can influence the interactions and processes within the organization and teams.

Some Examples

In the United States, a collaborative approach is often considered a desirable way for a project leader to lead a team. However, in various other cultures this approach can range from confusing (as in China) to being considered a sign of weakness in the manager (as in Malaysia).

From experience, I know that with some colleagues from India "yes" often means "I should not say no and contradict or offend you" rather than "yes, I will complete this task by the date you have asked for."

In Japan a nodding head often means "I hear and acknowledge what you are saying" as opposed to "I agree with the things that you are saying."

These and similar situations can impact the virtual global organization and teams in various ways. In the example of the US team leader using a collaborative style with a Malaysian team, the perceived weakness may lead to open disregard of the US person's leadership and a breakdown of the team.

Asking the team member from India for commitment to complete a task by the end of the week, receiving a "yes" in response, and then finding out on Friday afternoon that the task is not complete and that "yes" really meant "I did not want to tell you no just then or be disrespectful" can cause schedules to slip unexpectedly.

A team may discuss a topic during a video conference and assume that the polite head-nodding of the Japanese team member indicated agreement with a statement or perceived consensus, and then later receive information to the contrary that invalidates that assumption or the consensus.

Americans – Pay Attention

People from the United States have had a reputation for not working effectively with other cultures as well as parochial tendencies. Factors for this include the sheer size of the United States, its geographic isolation, large domestic markets, and the pervasiveness of English as a primary global language of business, relieving many Americans of the need to learn other languages and cultures.

Americans are becoming steadily more worldly, but also continue to believe in the superiority of American culture and methods. Americans are often perceived by other cultures as good at the technology and related issues, but not as effective with people and people-related issues across cultures.

Americans are known for wanting to "get down to business" versus building relationships. In most other cultures it is the opposite – relationship-building precedes serious business discussions.

Awareness of these perceptions and differences about themselves and other cultures will help the American leader or member of a global organization or team manage their behaviors and expectations effectively. Awareness of the effects of cultural differences is a first step to recognizing and managing these issues on a virtual team. The leader in such a situation must be aware of the countries and cultures represented on a team, assess for possible cultural issues, and then develop a plan for managing these.

For example, an American working with a team consisting of team members primarily located in France and Italy would be well-advised to temper their desire to jump right into business, push the schedule, or act informally – and do not expect a lot to be accomplished in the late July through August time frame – this is vacation season and much of Europe slows from a business perspective.

Take time to proactively consider, document and plan strategies for addressing cultural issues and demonstrate sensitivity and accommodation to the various cultures represented on the team. For the American, taking time to learn customs and practices of other cultures in the organization and on teams, and practicing and acknowledging these, helps to reduce the perception of Americans as insensitive to other cultures.

Become culturally aware – learn some things: The simple act of learning how to say and write a few simple phrases (greetings, thank you are perfect examples) in the languages used on your global team goes a long way toward demonstrating willingness to learn and communicate. The same goes for learning about specific holidays, customs, and other cultural elements. Most project team members will appreciate this effort. Dan McCarthy notes that one must be sure to hold the entire team to the same standards of accountability while also being culturally sensitive (McCarthy, 2009).

Know what you are saying: Be aware of the slang phrases, sport metaphors, and other things you may be used to saying. Purge them from your vocabulary when working with international groups. Know the meanings of words and phrases in other languages and countries. Great stories emerge when someone tells a group of people that they are "hot", meaning to express that they are too warm, when in fact the words they use convey an entirely different meaning in another language or vernacular.

Behavioral characteristics of effective and influential global leaders

The following traits apply to any leader in any setting. In chapter 30 of their 2000 book *Coaching for Leadership*, Maya Hu-Chan, Jeremy Solomons, and Carlos Marin identified five particular characteristics of effective and influential global leaders:

Trustworthy – Viewed as dependable and sincere. Keeps promises and displays an effective moral compass. Unafraid to lose a project if it compromises their integrity.

Respectful and caring – Shows respect for the dignity and worth of all and shows genuine interest in learning about other cultures while showing cultural empathy.

Balanced between doing and being – Recognition that, in some cultures, *who* a person *is* can be as or more important than *what* they can *do*; recognizes work/life balance differences across cultures.

Emotionally literate – Capable, especially under stress, of understanding where their reactions come from and managing their responses accordingly.

Culturally self-aware – Capable of recognizing and learning from the expectations associated with roles as defined by other cultures, as well as recognizing and effectively dealing with culturally influenced attitudes, values, and expectations. Examples include power, competition, perceptions, and use of time, individualism versus collectivism, formality, and structure (Adapted from Hu-Chan et al., 2000).

Summary

In this chapter we've discussed the importance of remote distributed communications and operational practices and tools. We discussed the importance of good and consistent training, and practices with new tools prior to using them for important events. We discussed the importance of ensuring a common and good experience for everyone, regardless of location, and what this means from a culture and tools perspective. We dug deeper into the role that culture and communications plays in successful remote distributed organizations and work, and noted that for global organizations, the awareness and respect for cultural differences and norms is critical.

In the next chapter, we will discuss the advantages and ramifications of success in remote distributed organizations and how to leverage success for growth and improvement.

CHAPTER 7

Remotely Successful

Success Is Self-Perpetuating

Technology and the global economy have been two primary drivers of the expanding prevalence of remote work and distributed organizations. As these types of organizational and work models continue to demonstrate success, technology has enabled and also been driven by these models and successes.

Another driver of remote distributed work models is the changing demographics of the global workforce. Younger workers have grown up with enabling technology and remote work options and now take them for granted. They expect to find remote options and the supporting technology in the workplace and arrive already knowing how to be effective without specialized technology training or concerns that things may not work as expected based on decades of on-site work habits – these "old" habits and expectations are simply not there for the younger members of the workforce.

Often, these legions of younger workers push the boundaries of organizations who must balance the desire to provide remote work options and support them with the latest tools for collaboration and productivity against the prevailing organizational culture as well as critical needs for security and

Chapter 7 | Remotely Successful

supportability. These same younger workers also expect a greater balance between their professional and personal lives, and remote distributed work and teams and tools help to provide this balance.

All of these factors combine to raise the expectations and demands for the increased use of remote work and virtual teams. Think of it as a self-perpetuating circle: The easier it is to collaborate as a remote member of a virtual/distributed organization, the more successful these models are. The easier it is, and the more successful these types of teams and organizations are, the more is expected of them, thus demanding more innovation in the tools and techniques which in turn yield more and better results (see Figure 7-1).

Figure 7-1. The self-perpetuating circle of collaboration and success

Lessons from the Global Experiment

This book opened with a short history lesson and a discussion of the lessons learned from the 2020 global Covid-19 pandemic, which forced (*or depending on your viewpoint, provided an opportunity for*) many organizations to experiment with remote and distributed work scenarios. It would be naïve to say or assume that all were successful – however, plenty of organizations did experience success. Some found they were able to operate in remote modes far more efficiently than they would have expected and found that many roles in their organizations could be performed remotely and quite effectively in this model.

The sudden removal of the daily commute provided flexibility and more productivity for many. Various studies and anecdotal data indicate that for some organizations and types of work, productivity increased with remote work arrangements. Many people expressed that the elimination of a commute enables them to devote more morning and evening time to exercise, meditation, family, and other personal pursuits, which in turn finds them at their home/remote workstation more refreshed, less stressed and therefore more productive, creative and collaborative – all elements that contribute to successful outcomes.

Success Perpetuates Freedom and Opportunity

People and organizations who deliver a successful experiment gain the freedom and opportunity to push further. A scientist who runs a successful experiment will push on to the next; a leader who tries a new approach to a business problem and is successful will gain the credibility and confidence to scale this model. The same is true with remote and distributed work and organizations.

Organizations who opt to continue remote distributed models for working after the Covid-19 period will experience varying levels of success due to a myriad of factors. Those who do experience success will extend and expand these models to more people and parts of their organization. They will also expand their specific definition of "remote," perhaps moving to a broader geographic area for recruitment and hiring or enabling people to work in a total remote mode versus a hybrid or flex option. Organizations may move up Mullenweg's model of distributed work autonomy and find that as they do so, they experience more success than they did when operating in full on-site mode or at level one or two.

Success – Recruiting and Hiring

Earlier in the book and in this chapter, we discussed how remote distributed organizations greatly expand their options for recruiting and hiring, truly fulfilling the interest to hire the best people no matter where they live. As this vision manifests, HR departments and hiring managers will experience success and provide organizational value in recruiting and hiring these remote workers, not only because they are no longer geographically limiting the candidate pool but also because the recruitment costs less – both in time and money – for the organization as well as the candidate, with no or minimal travel involved and less lost time for the candidate in their current job or other life commitments.

Fewer or no geographic restrictions also means that organizations will face fewer obstacles to becoming more diverse. With geography and the assumption that workers would need to be local no longer a factor, organizations pursuing diversity in their workforces for the various benefits that a diverse workforce brings will find success – not only in fulfilling the core objective of increased diversity, but also through the increasing success and performance that a diverse workforce is proven to bring to organizations.

Example – Automattic's Global Employee Base

As Matt Mullenweg puts it, the "hire the best people no matter where they live" approach enables the organization to leverage the vast majority of global talent that is located somewhere other than near one of your current physical locations. The money saved on recruiting and through employee retention can be reinvested in better training, benefits, and other value-creating elements (Mullenweg, 2020).

Mullenweg's Automattic is one of the best illustrations of this approach. In addition to WordPress, Automattic delivers ten other web-based products including WooCommerece and Tumbler. As of this writing, Automattic claims over 1300 people in 77 countries. Fully remote and distributed since inception in 2005, Automattic's ongoing growth, product development, and acquisitions certainly speak to the success of the totally remote and distributed organizational model inclusive of recruiting from a global talent pool (Automattic.com/about, 2020).

Example – CloudCraze's Instant Remote QA Team in California

2014 was an interesting year for CloudCraze. We had successfully implemented our cloud-based ecommerce system for several well-known customers and had others in process and in the sales pipeline. One of those was Pono, classic rock star Neil Young's short-lived high-quality digital music device and company. We'd landed Pono largely because Neil Young and Salesforce founder and CEO Marc Benioff had neighboring estates somewhere in Hawaii. When Neil Young asked his neighbor about ecommerce for his Pono product, one thing led to another, and we landed the deal.

By mid-2014 we were implementing the ecommerce site for the Pono music device while also building the equivalent of iTunes in three months, and we started to have software quality issues. Pono's VP of technology hit us pretty hard on our increasing bug rates, so we had to act quickly. CloudCraze founder and CEO Bill Loumpouridis used his connections to find us a great team of software quality assurance (QA) people, all based in California. Given our remote distributed model, we were able to rapidly add them to our team and our development processes to quickly reduce bugs in our core product. **Note** – I did not actually meet any of the new QA team in person until November 2015!

Success – Living There, Working Here

If you have never worked in an organization where your coworkers are distributed across a country or even globally, it is hard to wrap your mind around the idea that the person or people you work with most frequently live in other time zones and climates. I adjusted to this during my time at Promega from 2005 to 2012, when project team members were often from offices in Germany, Benelux, Australia, and elsewhere, and then gained further experience and comfort with this model during my CloudCraze days with the company and my coworkers spread across the United States and our customers located around the world.

During the Covid-19 pandemic, plenty of people took the opportunity to live and work someplace other than where they *had* been living and working. Earlier, I wrote about the exodus from places like San Francisco, New York, Silicon Valley, and other crowded and expensive regions. This manifested as the workers, realizing that as long as they would be working remote, they had no work-based ties to these areas, decided to try a different lifestyle for a while.

In my own organization and within my circle of contacts, people moved to bucolic northern Wisconsin and Door County, while others moved to Texas or Miami to be closer to family, to San Diego for the winter, or took their families on a temporary hiatus to the Rocky Mountains. I personally decamped to Arizona for a block of time. Stories like this played out all over the world.

When an organization tries this and finds that things don't fall apart just because people are not in the same physical space, and in fact people are happier with more of their personal as well as professional needs met (*remember Maslow and Herzberg?*), this success creates more willingness and opportunity to make this a permanent part of the organizational model – success perpetuates success.

Ongoing success with the remote model helps this to become a perfectly normal and seamless experience and expectation. In one case, I was interacting with an executive who had moved to the mountains and had been there for several months before sharing with me that they were actually living and working outside of Wisconsin – nothing in our interactions had made this evident. This same leader encouraged me to take advantage of the opportunity to live and work in a warmer place for the Wisconsin winter – this was indication of the confidence through success that the remote model had created for us both.

Success – Collaboration

Remote distributed models enable successful collaborations between organizations and people in different places, different companies, and different countries. Examples include research and development within companies, between multiple companies, global research alliances, product development, and software implementations.

Example – Collaboration with a Russian Crime Lab

In 2011, I was a project manager at Promega Corporation in Madison, WI. I was leading a project to develop software for an automated genetic identity workflow – the software would amplify and normalize the signal from human DNA to improve the function of laboratory automation tools. The project team included people on our Madison campus as well as from a crime lab based somewhere in Russia. Input from the Russian team, which would be the first pilot installation site, was critical to ensuring the software met the needs of professional crime lab managers and technicians.

At various points in the development process, input from the lab team in Russia included run-through of live installation and testing of the installed software working with the laboratory automation systems. By using conferencing software to share computer desktops, participants could see everything that was happening on the pilot installation and the Madison team could guide and assist the team on the ground in Russia. We also recorded the collaborative conferences for future use. This remote distributed partnership was critical and a key to the successful development of this software, as input from the Russian pilot lab enabled further development of the final commercial release of the software and DNA testing workflow, which included reagents and other Promega products that had to work with systems from various lab automation manufacturers.

Example – CloudCraze: Collaborating with Integration Partners

Growing CloudCraze from a few US customers to a global B2B ecommerce product meant partnering with global system integrators (SIs) like Accenture as well as regional system integrators like YourSL (now part of Salesforce) in Germany. YourSL brought us into the conversations with Coca-Cola Germany in late 2013, and by February 2014 we were in three-way negotiations with YourSL and Coca-Cola Germany to develop their first B2B ecommerce system.

On-site kick-offs and subsequent visits to Berlin helped to build relationships and collaboration. In one of the best examples of relationship-building I have experienced, YourSL's engagement leader gave a small group of us a tour of

Berlin's most famous places in a couple of hours prior to a dinner meeting the night before the project kick-off meeting. That attempt at relationship-building did not mean things always went perfectly.

Prior to ultimately building and implementing a successful ecommerce system, the three remote teams needed to work through various issues and obstacles. My attempts to speak some German probably helped a bit — these attempts at least amused my German colleagues. More critically, the total commitment of CloudCraze to keeping the project alive when YourSL lost confidence in the project was due to the good relationship we had forged with Coca-Cola Germany's CIO.

Once past the rough spots in the partnership and with responsibilities for data, functional development and front-end/user experience development sorted out, the three remote companies and their teams collaborated to deliver an ecommerce experience that was one of the highlights of Salesforce's annual Dreamforce conference in October 2014.

Success – Results

When remote and distributed teams start shipping product, finishing projects, and maintain and accelerate productivity, and further, find that they are happier working this way, the results speak for themselves. Sometimes external or internal customers need to see results to be convinced that the remote distributed model will work for them. Whether through quantitative or qualitative results and examples, there is plenty of evidence that remote models are successful. The successes experienced in specific circumstances and as a whole provide plenty of support for those organizations who are considering remote distributed scenarios as their Day One model and for those who are moving to this model as a permanent scenario.

Example – Telemedicine

Routine medical visits involve a lot of time and inefficiencies. In the United States, where most aspects of the visit have little to do with the actual reason for the visit and everything to do with ensuring an insurance company will pay for it and updating data in an Electronic Medical Record (EMR) system, the wasted time and built-in inefficiencies are stunning as well as frustrating. The Covid-19 pandemic forced many routine visits and many aspects of medical care to go fully online. Health systems and clinics enabled patients to update their own EMR prior to their visits and conducted many types of telehealth visits remotely. I personally participated in or witnessed several of these; most were quite efficient.

Qualitative and quantitative data support rapid acceleration of telemedicine adoption and capabilities in many regions, and one estimate posited that Britain's National Health Service had seen ten years' worth of change in less than a month as the pandemic forced providers to realize they could provide much of the healthcare experience remotely (Standage, 2020). There is every indication that the positive experiences and efficiencies in healthcare and telemedicine will sustain further success well beyond the end of the Covid-19 pandemic and become the norm.

There is nowhere in the world where success breeds more success than in the global capital markets, and remote distributed healthcare is a prime example. The success of telemedicine and the increase in healthcare provided through remote delivery during the Covid-19 pandemic is leading some to predict increasing investments in companies developing software, tools, and infrastructure to expand capabilities and options for remote and distributed healthcare. This could ideally lead to more readily available healthcare options for all, including in underserved areas and for underserved populations (Hall, 2020).

Example – Online Call Centers

Lots of jobs have *long* been doable by remote workers who need nothing but a telephone, a computer, and reliable Internet service. Call center operations are one example. Physical call center locations are very expensive; I learned this first-hand while implementing ecommerce for a one of Coca-Cola's US bottling groups. The remote distributed project that digitized this experience helped that particular Coca-Cola bottler lower its costs and increase its average order size, and this success prompted the bottler to invest in further projects. Not only was the project a financial success, but several of the project's leaders earned promotions as a result.

Any project and success that can improve the productivity of call center employees and lower the overall cost is a bottom-line benefit to the employer. Doctoral students at Harvard studied the performance of call center workers from early 2018 through August 2020 and found that on-site workers who switched to a remote work option increased their productivity by 7%, increasing by an additional 7.6% during the 2020 lockdown. These results and similar results from other studies and companies prompt the question as to whether remote work in these types of roles should be the norm, given the quantifiable productivity gains (*The Economist*, 2020).

Example – CloudCraze

In 2012 and 2013, CloudCraze continued to acquire more big-name customers for its ecommerce system. As with many other types of IT projects, ecommerce system implementations often involved sending a team of consultants to work with the clients at a specific client site. In these instances, many organizations and their clients expect the delivering organization and its partners (when necessary) to place consultants at the client site for weeks if not months – putting "butts in seats" and billing hours on-site until the ecommerce system goes live. This is not only expensive for the customer, since they are responsible for the travel costs and out-of-pocket living expenses for these consultants, but it is also taxing on the delivering organization as their people spend weeks and months away from their homes and families. Over time, this (in my experience) can lead to lower productivity and worker satisfaction.

CloudCraze realized early on that this approach was not efficient and would be expensive for clients as well as taxing on the morale of the staff who had to be away from home and travel every weekend. We also realized that it would also limit CloudCraze's ability to scale, as the implementation team was relatively small at that time and needed to be able to work on multiple implementations simultaneously in order to achieve growth – not something you can do with your team's butts in clients' seats at their physical locations.

Some clients were initially reluctant to allow CloudCraze to implement our hybrid delivery model, which involved remote preparations, a kickoff week of on-site work followed by several weeks or months of remote work with periodic on-site visits if and when necessary. The delivery team would come back on-site in the preparation for and performance of the critical system go-live. After a few successful implementations using this model, CloudCraze could point to it during the sales process as our standard implementation practice. With multiple successes and client references, we got much less pushback from prospective clients.

Since the CloudCraze implementation consultants were not constantly on the road and could have better work/life balance, CloudCraze was able to retain its core software delivery team while scaling and growing the organization, which in turn led to us acquiring more customers and improving delivery efficiency. Once again, success with remote models led to more success.

Not every customer was onboard with this hybrid remote/on-site model, and their projects sometimes suffered as a result. In one case, the customer's ingrained organizational culture kept them from seeing that the project and our team could be successful working remotely, and so they insisted on more physical presence from our teams. The result was a drop in day-to-day productivity – with the lead architect and developers from our team physically on-site, the client's lead felt free to interrupt their work constantly to ask questions, harangue them about progress, share unfounded worries, and generally create an unproductive and toxic situation. With this particular customer, we were able to work out a combination of periodic on-site work by the lead architect with the remainder of the team remaining in remote status except for user acceptance testing (UAT) and go-live.

Success and Expectations

Success, as noted at the start of the chapter, breeds success. People and teams that find success working in remote distributed scenarios will expect more of the same and will continuously innovate to enable this success. Organizations who experience ongoing successes with remote work models will clear any remaining barriers and doubts and begin to further enable these models and the people who both support and benefit from them.

As momentum increases and final reservations around remote distributed models of work fade, and the process and tools are continuously optimized to facilitate these models, expectations for success and accomplishments will go up. The demand for continued innovation from within the organization and from the providers of processes and tools will increase.

The overall expectations of remote distributed work on the part of the people doing it and the organizations engaged in it will increase. The expectations of technology capability, accommodation from employers, and expectations of productivity and achievement will continue to rise as these same people and supporting structures and technology improve their performance. Without a lot of empirical data as of yet, I'll still make a comparison to Moore's Law – the famous hypothesis from Intel founder and semiconductor icon Gordon Moore. Much like Dr. Moore correctly hypothesized that the rate at which transistors could be placed on a single unit of silicon would increase at a sustained rate for decades, I believe that the successes of remote workers and the technology that supports remote work will sustain gains in both the acceptance of and productivity of remote work.

Summary

In this chapter we reviewed how success in various aspects of remote and distributed working models will build upon themselves and provide momentum to organizations, the people using these working models, and the companies supplying the platforms and tools to enable this work. We discussed how ongoing success will foster and encourage further adoption and experimentation, increase the capability and diversity of the workforces in distributed organizations, and enable people to live wherever it suits their needs while working for their employers of choice.

In the book's final chapter, we will review pros and cons and contemporary arguments for and against remote and distributed work models in the 2020s and beyond. With an acknowledged bias toward the pros versus the cons, I will outline how most arguments support the potential for remote work to be an option that will persist and expand throughout the 2020s and beyond.

CHAPTER 8

Remote Arguments

For and Against Remote Possibilities

At no point do I assume or recommend that remote work scenarios are perfect or even a fit for every organization or type of work. There are simply some types of work where you just have to be physically present to perform the job – this book assumes this is the case. More critically and germane to the points and perspectives in this book – from a culture and leadership perspective, there are some organizations that, for any number of reasons, are not suited to or would not find remote and distributed work scenarios appropriate.

Organizations with intrinsically high levels of mistrust between leadership and employees, or old-school managers who *claim* they trust their employees but don't feel comfortable unless they see them working, will have to deal with these attitudes and cultural issues before they can see gains from remote distributed work scenarios.

This chapter will discuss some broad reasons that may stack up points for or against the long-term adoption of remote work scenarios. I'll review contemporary research and literature that examines the pros and cons of retaining remote work models beyond the general end of the Covid-19 pandemic and summarize some of the findings. The intent is to look at both

© Shawn Belling 2021
S. Belling, *Remotely Possible*, https://doi.org/10.1007/978-1-4842-7008-0_8

sides of the discussion, but not to be unbiased – this book is unapologetically about and in favor of the possibilities for successful remote distributed working scenarios.

Remote Opposition

In 2020, at the height of the Covid-19 pandemic when almost any company that could was working in a remote model, Reed Hastings, CEO of Netflix, was widely quoted as saying that Netflix teams would return to physically working in the office 12 hours after a vaccine was approved (he later qualified that remark to something more realistic). The general takeaway from this statement and various articles that quoted the information is that Hastings and his Netflix culture are not fans of nor a good fit for long-term remote work (Kelly, 2020).

The reasons for Hastings' opposition are not as important as the basic fact that the cultures that exist in many organizations will resist or are simply not conducive to a remote distributed work model. A quote from famous management consultant and author Peter Drucker, repeated countless times, notes that "culture eats strategy for breakfast." Remote distributed work models are no exception. It is even possible for a changing culture to evolve from one that supports or is foundational to remote distributed scenarios to one that rejects or limits the potential of remote work.

Remote Distrust

As I documented in earlier chapters, CloudCraze had been built from its inception as a remote distributed company. Fast-forward to early 2015, a year and a half after its acquisition by a Chicago investment group. The new CEO had changed the culture rapidly from the original remote distributed-first culture to a culture that valued having butts in the seats of the downtown Chicago office unless your job required you to be on the road or was a regional position.

In this new culture that put a premium on face time in the Chicago office, the CEO's distrust of the remote software development team grew for reasons that were particular to this culture and leadership style. He could see the outbound sales team smiling and dialing from their bullpen across the room, but he could not see the software development team that (with a few exceptions) were remote and distributed across the country. When one senior architect (note – this was a guy that the CEO had personally brought into the company when it was acquired) decided to move from a location on the METRA line to a country location closer to family, the CEO was furious, assuming the move was solely so that this architect could avoid coming into the office.

Such is culture and the tone that can be set by leadership. The emerging distrust of the development team's remote distributed model caused some morale issues and confusion within the remote development team. The coda to this example is that CloudCraze was ultimately acquired by Salesforce in 2018. Salesforce has a robust culture of remote work that was made even more so during the Covid-19 pandemic, with Salesforce expecting over half of its workforce to remain in a remote and flexible working mode (McLean, 2021). Things have likely changed for the better at CloudCraze, now known as Salesforce B2B Commerce. As Global Workplace Analytics put it, "the sweatshop and typing pool mentality has to be abandoned" (2021).

Culture

The Covid-19 pandemic forced (or, if you prefer, provided an opportunity for) organizations to test remote and distributed work models and assess how these fit within existing cultures as well as assess the influence on a culture that these models have. The Netflix and CloudCraze examples are both scenarios where, due to the strongly held attitudes of senior leaders, remote work was not likely to retain long-term traction. Other organizations have had different experiences, and many will retain and evolve remote and distributed work models in various forms after the Covid-19 pandemic has subsided. As Microsoft CEO Satya Nadella put it in a video for Microsoft's Viva product as it launched in February 2021:

> *We have participated in the largest at-scale remote work experiment the world has seen and it has had a dramatic impact on the employee experience. As the world recovers, there is no going back. Flexibility in when, where and how we work will be key.*

Microsoft subsequently implemented remote and remote hybrid work options that enable employees to choose working from home, change locations, or do a hybrid of in-office and remote work (Dickler, 2021).

I was already testing what the culture would allow at Madison College prior to the pandemic. Our IT department had moved out of the main campus and across the street to temporary digs while our space underwent a year-long remodel. I was encouraging my leadership team and all of the department to try out Teams for remote collaboration to avoid running between buildings for meetings or driving in for a single meeting. This practice was beginning to take hold, and then the pandemic hit.

The Covid-19 pandemic forced colleges and universities like mine to test and adopt remote ways of working. As the pandemic began to show signs of a projected end, college leaders were revisiting work models and culture in preparation for a post-Covid scenario in which far more people will be able to work remotely some or all of the time if their specific jobs allow this. At the most senior leadership levels (in academia, this is usually the president or chancellor's inner circle), this includes the actions of successful adopters and supporters consistently lobbying leaders who are less willing to embrace a permanent move to the availability of remote work. This lobbying is far more effective with examples of positive outcomes and benefits.

Culture is critical to successful organizations. Organizations with toxic cultures suffer in many ways, and organizations with positive cultures want to preserve them and the things that enable the positive culture. Naturally, leaders looking to remote and remote/on-site hybrid models are concerned about any possible negative effects on culture and culture development. A Gartner article from January 2021 summarized research on this topic, supporting that remote hybrid work models won't negatively affect culture, and in fact, may contribute:

> *About one-third of remote or hybrid employees report their organization's culture has changed since starting remote work... most say for the better. Employees who report that culture has improved since starting remote work are 2.4 times more likely to report high employee engagement (Wiles, 2020).*

Remote Innovation

In California's Silicon Valley, where culture and innovation are inextricably linked, some venture capitalists believe that the culture of innovation is hard to recreate virtually. One concern is that in-person, ideas are quickly hashed out in front of a whiteboard and either improved or discarded. Some leaders question whether that can be done with the same speed and rigor over Zoom and with whiteboard software.

They may have a point, but the fact is that plenty of organizations did this type of remote innovation and collaboration successfully before and during the pandemic and will continue to do so. Successful and innovative companies will be those who can find and develop talent and culture while providing the best of the flexibility and options that remote scenarios offer (Baron, 2020).

Another area of innovation comes from IT. Organizations traditionally built around on-premise and in-office work experiences may find that they can rethink their spending on systems and subscriptions that were designed around this experience as more of their teams spend some or all of their time in remote distributed work scenarios (Silver et al., 2020). The flipside of this, of course, is that IT will need to innovate in different ways to support their colleagues who are now working and collaborating remotely while also improving their own collaborative efforts as a remote and distributed IT department. In my own organization we are referring to this as the "digital workplace." The premise is that, assuming a person has a device appropriate to their role along with sufficient and reliable broadband Internet access, the appropriate digital experience should be available to them no matter where they are working or learning.

Culture Matters

It is appropriate to think about the effect that remote distributed scenarios could have on organizational culture. Fully remote work scenarios can introduce challenges to the creation or assimilation of a workplace culture. There is no doubt that the casual and unplanned conversations that take place at a physical workplace create important and beneficial relationships and connections. It is hard to have coffee, lunch, or beers virtually, although it is (remotely) possible. As an Amazon software engineer hired during the pandemic and onboarded remotely noted,

> *Despite virtual happy hours and game nights with his new co-workers, trying to socialize with people he has never met in person is "really awkward."*

In addition to the relationships and the social component, creating relationships with potential mentors can also be more challenging. It is critical to understand that these relationships are not impossible to create in the remote setting. Rather, there are challenges that must be acknowledged and planned for (Dickler, 2021).

I know from first-hand experience that a group of people in a physical workspace who fight through a problem together and deliver a project together form the culture of the team, and these experiences form the building blocks of an organization's culture. This does not mean that successful culture development in the remote distributed scenario is impossible – it can and has been done successfully, and more organizations will find their way to establishing and building their cultures in remote distributed settings.

Intentional Culture

The key to successful culture development in the remote distributed world is to be intentional about it. To successfully build and extend a remote distributed model beyond its pure necessity during the pandemic, leaders must be intentional about maintaining what is good about the existing culture as they transition to a remote distributed or remote hybrid model. They must also see it as an opportunity to change things that were not good about the culture and accept that the culture will evolve – change is inevitable, and it is often forced upon people and organizations – as we learned in 2020.

I've discussed the ways to be intentional about remote culture earlier in the book. The key point here is to assess your current organizational culture as a pro or con to remote distributed scenarios in your particular situation and organization and determine if it is an impediment, or if in fact, remote will help improve the culture. You may have an important and singular opportunity to create a new and improved culture based on a remote distributed workplace and organization.

Productivity

The Covid-19 pandemic provided a global laboratory for experiments in the productivity of remote workers, teams, and organizations. Formal studies and anecdotal information provided plenty of support for the idea that remote workers were highly productive. The potential for productivity gains alone is a good reason to extend and enhance this model. When combined with flexibility, work/life balance, and overall increased job satisfaction and improved employee retention that comes with this, the support for extending and building upon remote work seems obvious.

Meetings ≠ Productivity

Many of the arguments and experiences around productivity during the Covid-19 pandemic had to do with how people experience remote work. Because many leaders and workers had no experience in a remote scenario, days rapidly became filled up with video conferences. While this initially helped to bridge the gap and change from an all-on-site model to remote distributed models (and likely made people look and feel busy), ultimately, this led to burn-out and, for many, declining productivity. As in any situation where one is booked in meetings during an entire day and has no focus time to complete heads-down work, one feels unproductive and exhausted.

For those workers for whom remote meant they were able to work on a schedule more suited to their natural rhythms and find the solitude that enabled them to concentrate on heads-down work, productivity clearly went up. Anecdotally, the software developers, database administrators, and security engineers in my IT department all reported higher productivity and higher levels of general job satisfaction when they were able to go to a completely remote model due to the pandemic's forced remote work scenario.

This was not the experience of my leadership team. Until we adjusted work routines to account for and reflect the differences in remote versus on-site meetings and working, my leadership team felt unproductive and burnt out, precisely because many substituted meetings for heads-down work time so that they would be perceived as busy and therefore productive. Whether physically in a workplace or working remotely, getting past the idea that "meetings equals busy equals productive" is critical, and even more so in remote distributed scenarios.

An article in *The Economist* notes that executives who spend on average 23 hours per week in meetings can increase their productivity by cutting this in half, partially through ascending to the higher levels of autonomous work as described in Chapter 6 – this means planning fewer meetings and assuming and enabling more asynchronous work to increase productivity. The pandemic experience and the evidence make a strong case for productivity opportunities among leaders in remote distributed scenarios (Bartleby, 2021).

Remote Can = Productivity

In Chapter 7, I discussed examples where call center employees delivered higher levels of productivity combined with lowered cost per call, per order and higher average order size. Global Workplace Analytics, a consulting firm focused on future models of work including remote and work-from-home models, adds further evidence and examples of productivity increases seen in remote models, including

- Data from major global organizations that shows teleworkers up to 40% more productive.
- Up to two-thirds of employers reporting increased productivity with teleworkers.
- Commute time often turns into additional work time for the organization and people working from home spending a few more hours each week in productive work.
- Companies as diverse as a global credit card company and a computer manufacturer reporting productivity gains of up to 45% from remote workers.

Increases in employee autonomy through greater asynchronous work models and fewer geographic barriers to collaboration also increase opportunities for innovation and collaboration (Global Workplace Analytics, 2021).

I've shared my own observations of sustained and increased productivity in IT settings. Much of the literature I read as part of my job supports this and provides further evidence and expectations of improved productivity and increased morale through remote work. Other CIOs have seen similar scenarios and expect this to be the case for the long term.

At Carnegie Mellon University, CIO Stan Waddell noted that remote work scenarios and support are now part of long-term planning since Carnegie Mellon discovered that remote workers are "effective and aligned to the mission." Waddell and Carnegie Mellon also found that the use of data obtained through various campus systems and infrastructure assists in determining where to allocate resources, whether further to support remote work and productivity in that model or to reallocate resources to the areas of physical space seeing increased use as a result of the change in the overall model. This same data assists other institutions and their leaders in finding ways to support productivity and efficiency. According to Waddell, these advances in productivity and supporting technology are here to stay (Wood, 2021).

Travel and Productivity

The Covid-19 pandemic put a tremendous dent in travel of all kinds, and business travel was no exception. As someone who has spent a significant part of my career doing business travel, I have something of a love-hate relationship with it myself. Business travel does not always equal productive time. Even though for over three decades we have had amazing and constantly evolving tools to enable the business traveler to be productive while traveling, the nature of business travel and the time and energy it consumes also takes away from productivity.

Forced to stop or curtail business travel, some organizations and their leaders realized that they did not have to get on planes to close deals or advance their projects. One executive claimed that they closed $2 billion in deals over Zoom calls after the pandemic forced a stop to their previous practice of getting on a plane to close much smaller deals. Many organizations saw the stop to business travel correlate to productivity and more work/life balance along with the sudden and massive decrease in costs associated with business travel. These outcomes demand that organizations carefully think about the possibilities before returning to business travel as usual (Matyszczyk, 2020).

Bill Gates asserts that business travel will likely reappear at 50% of what was typical prior to the pandemic as organizations assess actual results achieved through virtual meetings against the lower business travel costs seen during the pandemic (Gates, interview, 2020). Against that viewpoint, some airline CEOs maintain that video conferences can never replace face-to-face meetings. Interestingly, through 2020 and early 2021, these same airlines quietly reconfigured their flights and routes to favor leisure travel in the face of extended declines in business travel.

Opposing Viewpoints

There are plenty of people, pundits, consultants, and leaders who point to data and experiences that contradict claims of heightened productivity and improving cultures with remote work models. There are strong and successful organizational cultures built around on-site/in-person work and strongly held beliefs supporting concepts that nothing can replace in-person collaboration and face-to-face relationships. There is doubtless an element of truth to every one of these examples.

What Are You Guarding?

In many cases, there is also something to protect. I could not help but wonder, as I wrote this manuscript, how many of the examples and predictions against remote worker productivity came from organizations with holdings in commercial real estate. If remote work takes off as many hope and predict, the world of commercial real estate will have to adapt.

I made reference earlier to the example of electronic medical record (EMR) software giant Epic and their massive, fanciful campus in Verona, WI. CEO Judy Faulkner invested millions, if not billions of dollars, in this campus – there is no doubt that she wants to see it used, and increased embrace of remote work models at Epic certainly would not achieve that utilization.

A July 2020 article from consulting giant McKinsey & Company struck a generally negative tone regarding long-term remote working. Referencing now famous examples from Yahoo! CEO Marissa Mayer's famous edict ending remote work and similar scenarios from HP and IBM, the McKinsey article illustrates downsides of remote work coming to outweigh the advantages in the experiences and opinions of these very large organizations.

The McKinsey article further illustrates some very valid examples of the negative aspects of remote work situations. Discussing how in-person work alongside coworkers helps to build critical ties, reinforce the culture, and enable various social interactions that form the framework of the company, the writers also caution against allowing two separate cultures to emerge – the on-site culture and the remote culture (this is what began to happen at CloudCraze after the 2015 acquisition, as discussed earlier in the book). While illustrating the challenges, the McKinsey team describes a variety of scenarios we accept as typical while working on-site and notes that the wise organization and its leaders will be mindful and intentional about re-creating these opportunities in remote settings (Alexander, De Smet, and Mysore, 2020).

Onboarding Can Be Challenging

Onboarding and assimilation, along with mentoring new employees can certainly be more challenging in remote and distributed situations. Without the automatic proximity of new coworkers to answer questions and provide assistance while also mentoring new people in practices and cultural norms, onboarding can be downright daunting.

One colleague of mine had to onboard several employees during the pandemic. The nature of the work – clinical research – made onboarding that much more challenging. Without existing processes to ensure new people got what they needed – everything from their laptop to building access and hands-on instruction of clinical practices – this onboarding experience was less than optimal. Discussion and analysis of this specific situation yielded some opportunities for improvement and application of remote work, but many aspects of this and similar jobs must be performed in-person and are best learned by watching another experienced practitioner.

As discussed in earlier chapters, the onboarding experience and tech support practices must continue to evolve to ensure that remote workers have what they need to be effective and to provide an experience that is the same as they would have in the office or on campus.

Innovation Challenges

Innovation in certain areas and fields is doubtless more challenging in remote scenarios. One example comes from technology hardware development. It is challenging for a group of engineers to pass around a prototype while examining and debating the layout of circuitry without physically holding this prototype and being in the same space. Remote collaboration platforms have yet to solve for this tactile experience.

The sense that a lack of spontaneity seen in remote and distributed environments compared to on-site colocated could impact creativity and innovation is a real concern. One engineer notes that their profession is not necessarily geared toward preparing presentations for scheduled online meetings as opposed to debating technical ideas in person. Some tech workers express the sense or assumption that presentations require more polish when they take on the feeling of a broadcast or a webinar as opposed to a whiteboard discussion or run-through of a slide deck with a small group in a conference room (Baron, 2020).

Collaboration Challenges

The whiteboarding experience is considered by many to be a centerpiece of collaboration, especially in technical environments. The stereotypical vision of a group of technical people gathered around a whiteboard and a conference table debating and illustrating, or sometimes simply staring at what is already on the board while deep in thought, is a vision that many associate with collaboration. Remote work scenarios introduce potential challenges to recreating this experience.

Collaboration tools and platforms have made tremendous advances in helping remote workers and teams collaborate effectively. Long before the pandemic, these tools enabled organizations like CloudCraze to run successful meetings and working sessions with teams distributed across the United States and across the globe. During the pandemic, the purveyors of these tools accelerated the pace of development and innovation to add more and more capabilities to enhance collaboration between workers who had no choice but to work remotely. These enhancements will enable remote workers, teams, and organizations to continue this collaboration as remote and remote hybrid workforce models expand.

One area of collaboration that is more challenging to recreate through technology platforms is sometimes known as *passive collaboration*. When we set up meetings with an agenda and with the intent of solving a problem during a specified period of time with pre-distributed artifacts and subsequent meeting notes, we are engaging in active and planned collaboration. The tools and platforms that have been in place for decades and saw rapid evolution during the pandemic are very good at supporting active collaboration.

Some argue that passive collaboration is as important if not more important to innovation. This takes us back to the whiteboard scenario, as well as invoking those references from previous chapters to unplanned and serendipitous encounters with coworkers in physical spaces that sometimes lead to "a-ha" moments. There are some who contend that the same tools which are effective at enabling and supporting active collaboration are less so at fostering passive collaboration. The very fact that a Zoom session must be planned in advance takes something away from the opportunity for unplanned or spontaneous collaboration happening because of people occupying the same physical space or sharing the same whiteboard at different moments (Shroff, 2021).

It is critical for leaders planning to extend their remote workplaces to consider hybrid meeting spaces that leverage technologies and platforms to recreate, as much as possible, these unplanned and passive collaboration scenarios. Earlier in the book I described how as of this writing my team and I were reimagining the final design for our remodeled spaces. One of our challenges and important objectives is creating hybrid meeting rooms that can support scenarios where people both on-site and remote are able to collaborate effectively in active and passive ways. You will find a plethora of technologies and platforms to consider when designing this capability into your remote distributed or remote hybrid workplace and culture.

Teaching and Learning

Having taught for decades in both classroom and online settings, I would be the first instructor to express a preference for certain types of classes to spark lively dialogue and engagement in-person versus online. One Carnegie Mellon instructor teaching a class on innovation noted that the first semester of remote instruction during the Covid-19 pandemic had a very different feel compared to previous semesters. The instructor felt that students did not seem as collaborative as they did in previous semesters of in-class instruction, and that the lack of out-of-class collaboration had a discernable impact (Baron, 2020).

The Covid-19 pandemic forced me to teach a number of classes and seminars online that I would ordinarily teach in-person. Through different formats and different platforms, I found varying levels of participant engagement, and with one particular group of technologists from the banking industry, I found it nearly impossible to spark engagement in the remote scenario. Given a choice, I prefer teaching these particular groups and seminars in-person.

However, many instructors have leveraged and will continue to leverage technology to overcome the lack of physical presence in a classroom. As with meetings, the technology to support different modes of instruction that do not rely on physical presence has long been in place, and it evolved rapidly during the pandemic. At my college, innovative instructors were experimenting with virtual reality (VR) classrooms well prior to the onset of the Covid-19 pandemic. Further investment and exploration in virtual reality technology enabled these instructors to recreate courses for nurses and emergency medical technicians as well as respiratory therapy technicians that previously were only taught with hands-on instruction. Augmented reality (AR), virtual reality, and hybrid classrooms will continue to provide evolving options for instructors at all levels of education to provide rich and engaging learning environments to remote distributed students and classrooms.

Theory X Workers

Sadly, it is not outside the realm of possibility that the greater autonomy that comes with remote work is too much of a temptation for people who lack discipline and dedication. This supports the Theory X concept that we discussed earlier in the book – the belief that people naturally avoid work and must be closely supervised and coerced to get it done. During the Covid-19 pandemic, some organizations and leaders doubtless experienced situations where newly remote workforces resulted in decreasing productivity, and scenarios where accountability and discipline declined (Levitt, 2020).

Broadly speaking, this viewpoint is heavily influenced by the nature of your organization, its work, and your workforce. Without going deep into examples, there is no question that there are types of work and work cultures that, for various reasons, have a reputation for people seeking the most possible compensation for the least amount of work. The danger lies in assuming this is the case for every person and every organization. If you work or lead in an organization like this, your problems existed long before remote and distributed work became a necessity and then a long-term option. You may not be in a position to realize the potential benefits of remote work, and pragmatic leadership demands that you honestly assess this before attempting to extend or implement a remote or remote hybrid work model.

My former software architect John, while a rockstar developer, also tended to use our remote distributed work environment to push the boundaries of what was acceptable regarding availability and responsiveness. I never learned to appreciate the game of "where's John?" when he was late for a client call or went off the grid for 36 hours at a time. You, too, may have a John in your remote workforce. Should that stop you from deploying this model? No, unless your organization is made up predominantly of people with this tendency. Again, this speaks to a hiring and culture problem as opposed to a remote versus on-site issue. If this is the case for you or your organization, fine-tune your hiring practices and give careful consideration to the type of culture you want to create before moving forward with your remote work model.

Theory Y Workers

Conversely, optimistic views of the post-pandemic world of work are a boon to people who are or believe in Theory Y – that work is a natural human endeavor and that people *want* to work for various reasons, including their own satisfaction and self-expression. Sometimes the skill set underpinning successful remote work is a natural thing where people can and do find their own personal rhythms and optimal ways of working. In other instances, new employee training and onboarding in remote scenarios will need to evolve to include techniques and best practices for remote work. Institutions like mine will need to add remote work etiquette and remote work micro-credentials to the curriculum.

Work in the 2020s: Remotely Different

This book has taken an overall optimistic tone about remote work and a presumption that as the Covid-19 pandemic of 2020 subsides in 2021 and organizations have the option of returning to their previous normal, most will not resume exactly as they were. The possibilities presented by remote distributed organizational models are too compelling to ignore. Technology, and a greater awareness of how unpredictable our world is, will combine with evolving flexibility and a greater understanding of the nature of work in the 21st century. This means that remote work and combinations of on-site and remote teams and organizations are where it's at for the foreseeable future. As leaders, we will learn, evolve, and bring the best from ourselves and our colleagues into the post-pandemic world of work.

As I reflect on the topics discussed in this book, the crucial elements that emerge are all about people. As a technology and project management leader, I've long lived by the maxim "people, process, then tools and technology." The approach to remote and distributed work is no exception. By focusing the majority of our energy on people and everything necessary to support them, we will find that we can and will design processes that accomplish this and select evolving tools that effectively support the people and the processes.

Many organizations and their leaders will need to change, and plenty will struggle and even step away from the challenge. In some cases, a long career of literally overseeing people while they work will be too much for some leaders to move away from, and that will be the tipping point for them to move on. Some organizations will find that their culture or the nature of their work or workforce is too resistant to the possibilities of remote and distributed work for various reasons.

The things that enable organizations and leaders to build the best teams and deliver the best outcomes will remain the same: hiring the best people, building trust and relationships, and focusing on positive cultures and supportive environments. These things are constant no matter what type of work environment we are in or hope to design. The technology and practices that we have discussed throughout this book are only supporting pillars to the core elements of people, trust, and positive cultures.

Leaders and organizations that successfully navigate the transition from a primarily on-site environment to a mix of remote and on-site, or even an all-remote model will find that motivation and success will sustain and advance progress. The examples provided by companies such as CloudCraze, Automattic, Collage.com, Basecamp, and countless other companies provide both inspiration and models for successful remote organizations and cultures. As I worked to wrap up this chapter in February 2021, I came back to it as two highly visible companies – Salesforce and Spotify – both announced that the concept of work as something you do versus a place you go and a specific time in which you do it are permanently emplaced well beyond the end of the Covid-19 pandemic. They join the ranks of organizations globally who learned through the pandemic that remote work options are an important component of their overall operating model.

In assessing and determining what is indeed remotely possible, I hope you find the ideas and information described here helpful and use them to make the coming years and the evolving global workplace productive and enjoyable for yourself, your teams, and your organization. It will be different, it will be challenging, and it will be remote.

CHAPTER 9

Epilogue

As I completed the final manuscript for this book in February and March of 2021, the possibility of returning to physical offices became an essential topic of discussion and media attention as the Covid-19 vaccine began to be widely distributed and the iron grip of the pandemic subsided. To generate the clicks, eyeballs, and traffic that lead to ad revenue and more data to harvest, some content creators and media channels stoked fear, uncertainty, and doubt regarding remote work and hybrid work.

The *Wall Street Journal,* for example, subtly catering (in my opinion) to the interests of its thousands of subscribers representing wealthy senior management and owners or leaseholders of vast tracts of office space, published articles questioning the long-term viability of remote work. One piece asked whether people knew when to stop working in remote settings. Another noted that many looked forward to resuming their daily commute. An ad for a luxury car brand showed a nicely dressed guy stepping into his gleaming vehicle, obviously relishing the chance to get behind the wheel and commute to work on what turned out to be empty, twisting roads (that's what all of our driving commutes look like, right?).

Business media widely shared the views of people like Goldman Sachs CEO David Solomon, who called remote work an "aberration" while questioning whether culture could be appropriately developed in remote settings and stating firmly that Goldman Sachs would be bringing staff back into the office as soon as possible (Jenkins, 2021).

At the other end of this spectrum, I found the Ford Motor Company who determined that post-pandemic, their workspaces would be reconfigured. Large numbers of their employees would be allowed to continue remote work and come into the office only as necessary. This was not purely a pandemic-inspired move: Ford had been considering options to consolidate and redesign their workspace, and, as with so many other companies, the Covid-19 pandemic simply accelerated these plans and forced a confirming experiment (Howard, 2021).

Remote Must Be Valued Same As In-Office

A topic that often emerged in the various articles I reviewed was a concern that employees who chose to come back into the office regularly would be valued or seen in a more positive light than those employees who continued to work remotely or work in a hybrid model. I know I am biased, but I sensed a subtle subtext in these articles, sowing fear and uncertainty among people who were likely looking forward to years of flexibility granted through permanent remote work options. Facing the question of whether or not one will be valued or promoted if one does not come back into the office permanently is frankly ridiculous in the 2020s.

Think about this: Countless people chose to work through the pandemic by changing where they lived or even uprooting themselves and turning into digital nomads. These people found that they could work from anywhere while experiencing an entirely different and more satisfying lifestyle. People with the courage to do this are the kind of people who are also likely to innovate, collaborate, and rise to challenges. Do you want to create a workplace where these people are valued less than their colleagues who come into the office regularly? The experience and talent of all cohorts of workers must be respected and supported regardless of physical location.

A major theme throughout this book has been how to build an organization that will be supportive and successful of the remote work model and, critically, the people who will be working remotely. It is essential to recognize the shift from simply offering remote work as an option to working in a model where the organization provides the appropriate support to ensure a common and level experience for everyone, whether working in the office or working remotely. The success of your organization throughout the 2020s will hinge upon your ability to leverage the reality of remote work as a valuable and permanent option while ensuring that everyone in your organization is appropriately supported and has a common and excellent working experience.

Writing for *Fast Company*, Harvey Deutschendorf (2021) noted that engagement is a huge issue for remote employees and that many workers would leave their current organization for a company that demonstrated more empathy. Recognizing the need to be empathetic to remote workers is critical to ensuring success as you transition to an all-remote or hybrid remote and distributed model. It is vital that leaders intentionally maintain contact with staff and never assume everything is OK. Sometimes the video camera can be helpful in allowing us to observe the expressions of our colleagues. At the time of this writing, my boss shared an anecdote about meeting with one of our colleagues and immediately knowing from her facial expression that she wasn't having a good day. Their agenda immediately changed to address this, and both later reported feeling better for the opportunity to have talked things through.

Writing for *Forbes Small Business Council*, Lee Shapiro referred to an unprecedented pace of change as employees everywhere faced the conclusion of year one of remote work and all of the learning that went with it. Shapiro expressed a belief that many companies will reduce physical office space and repurpose it for periodic gatherings intended to maintain connections as opposed to a daily workspace. Reaffirming contentions and findings I provided in earlier chapters, Shapiro referenced continued advances in ecommerce for retailers who may never have considered it and the pivot to healthcare and telehealth with more focus on the consumer (Shapiro, 2021).

Permanently and Digitally Enabled

At various points in previous chapters, I have referred to Salesforce and the experience I had working at CloudCraze – a company built totally on the Salesforce platform. Throughout 2020 and into 2021, Salesforce continued its tendency to be a very forward-thinking company in handling the pandemic's forced pivot to remote work. In my experience, Salesforce had always embraced and enabled a remote work-from-anywhere capability and culture. Founder and CEO Marc Benioff once claimed he could run the entire company from his smartphone. With the whole Salesforce infrastructure at his disposal, he has historically worked from his various homes and offices, and most Salesforce employees have long had this flexibility.

In late February 2021, Salesforce's Chief People Officer Brent Hyder announced that its new, permanent model meant that the "9-to-5 workday is dead" (Roche, 2021). Salesforce then chose to cancel its plans to lease large amounts of office space in a new San Francisco building (McLean, 2021). Another Salesforce executive, Peter Coffee, wrote of the return to the "digitally enriched" office, noting that the most significant difference in the world enabling permanent change in our working habits was the availability of bandwidth to massive numbers of people.

Coffee's point was that designated workplaces had existed for hundreds of years for a reason – that's where the equipment was, that's where the information was kept, and for hundreds of years, the working model of legions of clerks and workers under one roof supervised by executives in private offices made some sense. However, as technology evolves, people find that the "office" doesn't need to be defined by a physical location. In fact, the opportunity to work from a place designated by the *worker* provides many opportunities to save time and be more productive and enrich their lives. According to Coffee, the concept of returning to reimagined workspaces enabled by digital tools and bandwidth meant that "this time, things really will be different" (Coffee, 2020).

Taking this a step further, Microsoft announced in March 2021 the creation of a technology called *Mesh*. The concept behind Mesh is use of virtual reality (VR) to enable workers to digitally interact in a shared virtual space while remaining physically remote. Microsoft believes that this technology could transcend the obstacles faced by remote workers by enabling a type of shared space and shared interaction. Granted, this technology demands substantial compute power and bandwidth, and the assumption that workers will sign up to wear VR goggles for extended periods. However, given the experience at my own college, where instructors have created rich classroom experiences using VR, the possibilities are definitely there (Microsoft, 2021).

This Is Not Disruption

Microsoft also posted social media content referring to hybrid models of working where some staff is in the office, and others work from home as a "great disruption." Microsoft correctly identified that these flexible options became permanent, and the environment in which companies must compete for talent significantly changed. The long-term experiment created a more global and fluid marketplace for talent and work, and every organization was forced to respond and adapt (Microsoft, 2021).

The thing Microsoft got wrong about this was thinking of it as a *disruption*. Many organizations have been successfully working in a remote or hybrid remote model for decades, and the Covid-19 pandemic simply forced many more organizations to experiment and learn. Instead of thinking about this as a disruption, it is critical to think of this as a huge opportunity to innovate and iterate ways of working that offer productivity, flexibility, balance, and relationship building, all while enabling organizations to hire their best people regardless of location. Organizations and their leaders who can do this and build a winning culture based on a remote or remote hybrid work model will be the most competitive throughout the 2020s.

As I reviewed dozens of articles from February and March of 2021, the emerging theme was that workers and employers learned and experienced far too many positive outcomes for remote work not to be a mainstay work experience and option for the foreseeable future. At the same time, another emerging theme was that remote work is not a panacea – for example, remote work options cannot magically make a toxic workplace better, nor can it substitute for emotionally and organizationally savvy leaders who are empathetic and interested in developing their people and their culture.

The gist of many articles conveyed recognition of practical issues that I've addressed previously in the book. There is no question that face-to-face interaction with other humans is critical – it helps us forge relationships and spurs creativity. At no point do I suggest that remote work eliminates that human need. Recall that in previous chapters, I devote significant verbiage to describing how to create that culture and how to ensure that periodic face-to-face gatherings are an essential part of your routine, whether starting from Day 1 as a remote company or instilling remote as an option for your organization.

Hybrid Remote Will Be the Order of Business

The consensus from my review of many articles was that businesses and organizations would adapt to an ongoing hybrid approach, combining periods of remote work with on-site work. Workplaces would reconfigure to place less emphasis on individual permanent office space and instead create flexible workspaces that accounted for workers' periodic presence and their need to collaborate, work at individual desks, and work elsewhere. These same spaces must and will be optimized to enable an excellent experience for people joining meetings remotely or in the room, with no distinction or degradation of experience or participation for those joining from a remote location.

The outcomes and learnings from the remote work experiment of 2020 – 2021 emerged in other areas. As of this writing, I teach several courses for universities across the United States. I teach a course focused on leading virtual and colocated project teams, and I also teach a course focused on leading and managing organizational change. In both courses, contemporary literature as well as real-life examples of how remote work as an enabler and catalyst for change and opportunity for innovation emerged.

One of my students discussed how remote work experience showed that remote meeting participation can enable productivity. This student worked in a laboratory environment and noted that she valued the ability to join a presentation from a phone or laptop as it enabled the ability to keep running a time-consuming lab procedure while still participating in the presentation rather than completely missing it. This student further noted that virtual meetings and remote work helped foster new ideas on boosting lab morale and collaboration.

Another of my students noted that remote and hybrid remote work options were indeed not revolutionary. He also commented that companies had to recognize that work flexibility from the office or home was something they had not considered when building their operations and technical infrastructure.

He also noted that one of the challenges of the 2020s would be how companies can appropriately quantify productivity through various metrics such as KPIs and OKRs.

Organizational Change Leadership and Education Will Be Needed

I wrote this book because I wanted to share my practical and theoretical knowledge on remote, virtual, and distributed organizations and work with people who are new to this and recognize it as a model, an approach that has traction and long-term benefits far beyond the Covid-19 pandemic. There is and will be an ongoing need for education and training specifically focused on the knowledge and skills needed to create the culture and organizational structure necessary to ensure remote work is a valuable and thriving component of an organization's operating model.

There is a corollary need for leadership and expertise in organizational change for companies shifting to permanent models of remote and hybrid remote and distributed working. Like any significant change, an intentional and permanent shift to a remote or hybrid remote and distributed working model requires all of the expected work and supporting structures typical to change. Creating a vision, getting buy-in, recruiting early adopters, ensuring leadership support, designing and executing the change inclusive of training and education, and then sustaining and making the new way of operating the permanent model are all critical components of shifting to a remote or remote hybrid approach.

As I write the last words of this epilogue, March 2021 is about to give way to April. Media and advertising are focused on the possibilities of return to life somewhat as we knew it before February 2020. One thing that will not look the same is the workplace. Remote distributed and remote hybrid modes of working have proven to be effective and beneficial and are here to stay.

The 2020s will see organizations globally figuring out how to make this option effective and productive and working through the necessary changes. Read this book carefully and apply the ideas and lessons and examples, and you will be one of those organizations that turns the global experiment with remote work into sustainable gains in productivity and employee satisfaction and ultimately a competitive advantage.

Collaborative Servant-Leadership Will Rule the 2020s

I'll close by referring one more time to leadership. Earlier I wrote of aspects of leadership that are not suited to success in a remote distributed or remote hybrid approach. Theory X managers, managers who must see butts in seats to believe work is getting done, leaders who focus on charismatic front-of-room styles – their day is long past. The collaborative leader who leads by example, supports others in completing work and removing impediments, who shows empathy and takes care of people – your stock is on the rise. Take the lead and show how it's done!

Leaders must embrace humility as the workplace evolves. The leader who is secure in themselves, who fosters positive culture, who celebrates the accomplishments of teams, who admits that they along with everyone is finding their way through the ongoing changes associated with new working models is the leader who will be effective and successful in the 2020s. I call this approach "collaborative servant leadership."

The leader who brings together the strengths of the people in their organization, offers a vision, then solicits feedback to improve and implement that vision, all while focused on removing impediments and enabling teams to do their best work is a collaborative servant leader. Leading while serving and insisting upon collaboration is the leadership model that will show the way as remote work with its various implementations and manifestations evolves through the 2020s. Be that leader. Good luck!

Bibliography

"Advantages of Agile Work Strategies For Companies." Global Workplace Analytics. Accessed January 12, 2021. https://globalworkplaceanalytics.com/resources/costs-benefits.

Alexander, Andrea, Aaron De Smet, and Mihir Mysore. "Reimagining the Postpandemic Workforce." McKinsey & Company. Last modified July 7, 2020. www.mckinsey.com/business-functions/organization/our-insights/reimagining-the-postpandemic-workforce.

Artiss, Dave. "The Automattic Hiring Process." David Artiss. Last modified June 30, 2020. https://artiss.blog/2019/03/the-automattic-hiring-process/.

Automattic. "About Us." Automattic. Last modified November 6, 2020. https://automattic.com/about/.

Baron, Ethan. "Silicon Valley's Million Dollar Question: Does Remote Work Kill Innovation?" *The Mercury News*. Last modified December 14, 2020. www.mercurynews.com/2020/12/13/silicon-valleys-million-dollar-question-does-remote-work-kill-innovation/.

Bartleby. "The Lockdown Has Caused Changes of Routine." *The Economist*. Last modified January 13, 2021. www.economist.com/business/2021/01/13/the-lockdown-has-caused-changes-of-routine.

Basecamp. "Getting Started | Basecamp Employee Handbook." Basecamp: Project Management & Team Communication Software. Accessed December 29, 2020. https://basecamp.com/handbook/09-getting-started.

Berkun, Scott. *The Year Without Pants: WordPress.com and the Future of Work*. Hoboken: John Wiley & Sons, 2013.

Bodenhorn, H. "Business in a Time of Spanish Influenza." NBER. Last modified July 2020. www.nber.org/papers/w27495.

Bibliography

Borders, Kevin. "The Secret to Building Trust in an All-Remote Startup." Medium. Last modified March 10, 2020. https://medium.com/swlh/the-secret-to-building-trust-in-an-all-remote-startup-8a7da79bfeba.

Coffee, Peter. "Why We'll Want to Go Back to the (digitally Enriched) Office." Diginomica. Last modified September 10, 2020. https://diginomica.com/why-well-want-go-back-digitally-enriched-office.

Cohen, Arianne. "The Surprising Traits of Good Remote Leaders." BBC page. Last modified September 9, 2020. www.bbc.com/worklife/article/20200827-why-in-person-leaders-may-not-be-the-best-virtual-ones.

Davidow, Bill. "Hooray for Marissa Mayer." *The Atlantic*. Last modified March 5, 2013. www.theatlantic.com/business/archive/2013/03/hooray-for-marissa-mayer/273694/.

Deutschendorf, Harvey. "5 Things Emotionally Intelligent Leaders Do to Retain Remote Workers." Fast Company. Last modified February 25, 2021. www.fastcompany.com/90608511/5-things-emotionally-intelligent-leaders-do-to-retain-remote-workers.

Dickler, Jessica. "For Better or Worse, Working from Home is Here to Stay." CNBC. Last modified March 11, 2021. www.cnbc.com/amp/2021/03/11/one-year-into-covid-working-from-home-is-here-to-stay.html.

The Economist. "Does Working from Home Make Employees More Productive?" *The Economist*. Last modified December 27, 2020. www.economist.com/graphic-detail/2020/12/27/does-working-from-home-make-employees-more-productive.

Fayard, Anne-Laure, John Weeks, and Mahwesh Khan. "Designing the Hybrid Office." *Harvard Business Review*. Last modified March 1, 2021. https://hbr.org/2021/03/designing-the-hybrid-office.

Ferrazzi, Keith. "How to Build Trust in a Virtual Workplace." *Harvard Business Review*. Last modified October 8, 2012. https://hbr.org/2012/10/how-to-build-trust-in-virtual.

Francis, Paige. "How 2020 Reprioritized Leadership Qualities And Why We Should Keep Them." *Forbes*. Last modified December 27, 2020. www.forbes.com/sites/paigefrancis/2021/12/27/how-2020-reprioritized-leadership-qualities-and-why-we-should-keep-them.

Gates, Bill. Interview. *Bloomberg One*. Bloomberg, August 4, 2020.

Gelles, David. "An Evangelist for Remote Work Sees the Rest of the World Catch On." *The New York Times – Breaking News, US News, World News and*

Videos. Last modified July 14, 2020. www.nytimes.com/2020/07/12/business/matt-mullenweg-automattic-corner-office.html.

Hall, Christine. "Forecast: Health Care In 2021 Will Focus On 'Digitization Of The Patient Experience'." Crunchbase News. Last modified December 30, 2020. https://news.crunchbase.com/news/forecast-health-care-in-2021-will-focus-on-digitization-of-the-patient-experience.

Howard, Phoebe W. "Ford to Eliminate Individual Desks for Many Workers After Pandemic Subsides." *USA TODAY*. Last modified March 19, 2021. www.usatoday.com/story/money/cars/2021/03/19/ford-jobs-pandemic-remote-work/4750060001/.

Hu-Chan, Maya. "4 Tips to Avoid a Communication Breakdown When Your Small Business Is Working Remotely." Inc.com. Last modified March 18, 2020. www.inc.com/maya-hu-chan/4-tips-to-avoid-a-communication-breakdown-when-your-small-business-is-working-remotely.html.

Hu-Chan, Maya, Jeremy Solomons, and Carlos E. Marin. "Becoming an effective global leader." In *Coaching for leadership*, 1–6. Jossey-Bass/Pfeiffer, 2000.

Hutchinson, Lee. "Going All-in on Remote Work: The Technical and Cultural Changes." Ars Technica. Last modified August 28, 2020. https://arstechnica.com/information-technology/2020/08/work-from-home-05-culture/.

Jenkins, Cameron. "Goldman Sachs CEO Slaps Down 'aberration' of Remote Work." TheHill. Last modified February 24, 2021. https://thehill.com/homenews/news/540376-goldman-sachs-ceo-slaps-down-aberration-of-remote-work.

Kelly, Jack. *Forbes*. Last modified September 8, 2020. www.forbes.com/sites/jackkelly/2020/09/08/netflix-ceo-reed-hastings-is-not-a-fan-of-working-from-home-and-wants-his-employees-back-at-the-office-12-hours-after-a-vaccine-is-approved.

Kropp, Brian. "9 Trends That Will Shape Work in 2021 and Beyond." *Harvard Business Review*. Last modified January 14, 2021. https://hbr.org/2021/01/9-trends-that-will-shape-work-in-2021-and-beyond.

Laker, Benjamin. "Here's Why Leaders Don't Want To Support Remote Working." *Forbes*. Last modified June 24, 2020. www.forbes.com/sites/benjaminlaker/2020/06/24/heres-why-leaders-dont-want-to-support-remote-working.

Lardinois, Frederic. "Microsoft Launches Viva, Its New Take on the Old Intranet – TechCrunch." TechCrunch. Last modified February 4, 2021. https://techcrunch.com/2021/02/04/microsoft-launches-viva-its-new-take-on-the-old-intranet/.

Bibliography

Levitt, Howard. "Howard Levitt: Working from Home Giving Rise to Insidious Trend — Time Theft by Employees." *Financial Post.* Last modified November 17, 2020. https://financialpost.com/executive/careers/howard-levitt-working-from-home-is-giving-rise-to-an-insidious-trend-time-theft-by-employees.

Matyszczyk, Chris. "Microsoft Just Revealed the Future of Teams (You May Love It, Airlines Won't)." Technology News, Analysis, Comments and Product Reviews for IT Professionals | ZDNet. Last modified March 6, 2021. www.zdnet.com/google-amp/article/microsoft-just-revealed-the-future-of-teams-you-may-love-it-airlines-wont/.

Matyszczyk, Chris. "United and American Just Got a Chilling Reality Check (from a Big Flyer)." ZDNet. Last modified October 24, 2020. www.zdnet.com/article/united-and-american-just-got-a-chilling-reality-check-from-a-big-flyer/.

McGregor, Jena. "Six ways your office will be different in 2021, assuming you ever go back to it." *The Washington Post.* Last modified December 30, 2020. www.washingtonpost.com/road-to-recovery/2021/01/03/rtr-officetrends/.

McLean, Tessa. "Salesforce Cancels Huge Downtown Office Lease in SF." SFGATE: San Francisco Bay Area – News, Bay Area News, Sports, Business, Entertainment, Classifieds – SFGATE. Last modified March 11, 2021. www.sfgate.com/bayarea/amp/salesforce-cancels-office-lease-san-francisco-16015817.php.

Microsoft. "The Next Great Disruption Is Hybrid Work—Are We Ready?" Microsoft. Last modified March 2021. www.microsoft.com/en-us/worklab/work-trend-index/hybrid-work.

Mullenweg, Matt. "Are We at the End of the "Culture of Presentism and Micromanagement"?" Distributed.blog. Last modified July 2, 2020. https://distributed.blog/2020/07/02/autonomy-enrique-dans-forbes/.

Mullenweg, Matt. "Distributed Work's Five Levels Of Autonomy." Matt Mullenweg. Last modified April 27, 2020. https://ma.tt/2020/04/five-levels-of-autonomy/.

Mullenweg, Matt. "Second-order effects." Matt Mullenweg. Last modified August 18, 2020. https://ma.tt/.

Nisen, Max. "THE END OF WORKING FROM HOME: Best Buy Kills Flexible Work Program." *Business Insider.* Last modified March 5, 2013. www.businessinsider.com/best-buy-ending-work-from-home-2013-3.

Pochepan, Jeff. "Here's What Happens When You Take Away Dedicated Desks for Employees." Inc.com. Last modified May 10, 2018. www.inc.com/jeff-pochepan/heres-what-happens-when-you-take-away-dedicated-desks-for-employees.html.

Bibliography

Quealy, Kevin. "The Richest Neighborhoods Emptied Out Most As Coronavirus Hit New York City." *The New York Times* – Breaking News, US News, World News and Videos. Last modified May 15, 2020. www.nytimes.com/interactive/2020/05/15/upshot/who-left-new-york-coronavirus.html.

Rad, Parviz F., and Ginger Levin. *Achieving Project Management Success Using Virtual Teams*. Plantation: J. Ross Publishing, 2003.

Roche, Julia L. "Salesforce Becomes a 'success from Anywhere' Company with Record Year." Yahoo Finance – Stock Market Live, Quotes, Business & Finance News. Last modified February 26, 2021. https://uk.finance.yahoo.com/news/salesforce-q-4-earnings-results-and-future-of-work-191112659.html.

Sarabyn, Kelly. "Why Did Leaders in Remote Work Curtail the Practice?" Building Successful Remote Teams Since 2018. Last modified December 18, 2020. www.acorn.work/why-did-leaders-in-remote-work-curtail-the-practice/.

Shapiro, Lee. "The unprecedented pace of change." *Forbes*. Last modified February 25, 2021. www.forbes.com/sites/forbesbusinesscouncil/2021/02/25/the-unprecedented-pace-of-change/.

Sheynkman, Aleks. "How Do You Calculate Space Utilization? Read These 9 Points." SpaceIQ. Last modified March 17, 2020. https://spaceiq.com/blog/calculate-space-utilization/.

Shroff, Mohak. "Passive Collaboration is Essential to Remote Work's Long-term Success – TechCrunch." *TechCrunch*. Last modified March 10, 2021. https://techcrunch.com/2021/03/10/passive-collaboration-is-essential-to-remote-works-long-term-success/.

Silver, Michael, Stephen Kleynhans, Leif-Olof Wallin, Chris Silva, Rafael Benitez, Dan Wilson, and Stuart Downes. "Quick Cost Cuts for Digital Workplace Infrastructure and Operations." Gartner. Last modified October 29, 2020. www.gartner.com/en/documents/3992484/quick-cost-cuts-for-digital-workplace-infrastructure-and.

Simons, John. "IBM, a Pioneer of Remote Work, Calls Workers Back to the Office." *WSJ*. Last modified May 18, 2017. www.wsj.com/articles/ibm-a-pioneer-of-remote-work-calls-workers-back-to-the-office-1495108802.

Standage, Tom. "New Technological Behaviours Will Outlast the Pandemic." *The Economist*. Last modified November 16, 2020. www.economist.com/the-world-ahead/2020/11/16/new-technological-behaviours-will-outlast-the-pandemic.

Bibliography

Stillman, Jessica. "In 2021, the 9-to-5 Will Become the '3-2-2,' a Harvard Business School Professor Predicts." *Inc.com*. Last modified December 16, 2020. www.inc.com/jessica-stillman/remote-work-schedules-harvard-professor-ashley-whillans.html.

Thompson, Derek. "The Workforce Is About to Change Dramatically." *The Atlantic*. Last modified August 6, 2020. www.theatlantic.com/ideas/archive/2020/08/just-small-shift-remote-work-could-change-everything/614980/.

Unikel, Jill. "How Salesforce Is Continuing To Deliver A World-Class Employee Experience." Salesforce News. Last modified August 27, 2020. www.salesforce.com/news/stories/how-salesforce-is-continuing-to-deliver-a-world-class-employee-experience/.

Wiles, Jackie. "No, Hybrid Workforce Models Won't Dilute Your Culture." Gartner. Last modified January 7, 2021. www.gartner.com/smarterwithgartner/no-hybrid-workforce-models-wont-dilute-your-culture/.

Wood, Colin. "Remote Work, Data Are Long-term Assets for Universities, Says CIO." EdScoop. Last modified January 28, 2021. https://edscoop.com/remote-work-data-university-covid19-stan-waddell/.

Index

A

Americans, 88, 89
Annual meeting, 47
Asynchronous communication, 84
Asynchronous work models, 35, 107
Audio-only conversation, 84
Automattic, 57, 71, 94
Awareness, 87, 88, 113

B

Basecamp, 58, 81, 114
Best Buy, 5, 6
Business media, 115
Business-to-business (B2B), 14
Business travel, 25

C

Call center operations, 98
CEO's perception, 31
Client assignment, 44, 56
Client delivery team, 7
Cloud-based storage, 10
CloudCraze, 70, 71, 81, 94, 96, 98, 99, 103
CloudCraze Software, 6, 11
Collaborations, 96, 110, 111
    approach, 87
    CloudCraze, 96, 97
    Russian crime lab, 96
    space, 20
    success, 96
    tools, 3, 76, 77
Collage, 15, 43, 48, 49, 57, 61
Collage.com, 15, 43, 71, 81
Commerce system, 14, 96–99
Communications, 51, 82
    benefits, 52
    connections, 53
    continuous asynchronous virtual meeting, 52
    technology, 53
Communication tools, 3, 52, 77
Conferences calls, 36
Covid-19, 9, 17, 25, 28, 95, 113
Cultural awareness, 87
Cultural elements, 89
Culturally self-aware, 89
Cultural norms, 49, 88, 112
Culture, 77, 89, 90, 103, 104
Culture space, 20
Customer relationship management (CRM), 3

D

Desk space, 21–24, 30
Develop curriculum, 56
Digital ninja, 79

Index

Digital workplace, 53, 104, 107
Digital work space, 81
Distributed vs. colocated workforce, 11
Distributed development teams, 8
Distributed remote model, 9
Distributed teams, 5, 6
Distributed workforce, 10, 12, 16, 53
Distributed working model, 17, 102, 120, 124
Distrust, 102, 103

E

EDL Consulting, 13, 14, 18, 23, 42, 44, 67
EDL culture, 47
EDL practices
    annual meeting, 47
    monthly all-hands, 47
Electronic Medical Record (EMR) system, 37, 97, 109
Empathy, 46, 48, 61, 121
Excellence in Delivery Leadership (EDL), 13
    remote distributed model, 14
    software product company, 14
Extroverts, 63–65

F

Fear of Missing Out (FOMO), 46, 76
Feedback loop, 57
Five-level model, 85, 86
Freedom, 85, 93
Fully remote organizations, 24, 45

G

Geographically distributed teams, 3, 4
Global communication, 2
Global experiment, 38, 92, 124
Global workplace, 103, 107, 114

H

Hallway encounters, 5
Hand-held supercomputer, 36
Hawthorne Effect, 3

Hiring, 43, 93
    Collage.com, 43
    interview questions, 43
    learning, 44
    remote/virtual scenarios, 43
    specific project/client assignment, 44
    trust, 42
Home office, 10, 14, 15, 23–25, 33, 37
Humans, 20, 22, 65, 123
Hybrid in-office/remote work schedules, 34
Hybrid model, 105, 116
Hybrid organization, 50
Hybrid remote work, 119
Hybrids, 72
Hybrid workforce, 22, 111

I, J

In-crowd, 76
Information-based business, 2
Innovation, 110
In-office model, 20
In-person all-hands, 61
Intentional culture, 105
Internet, 2–4, 10, 37, 105
Internet Relay Chat (IRC), 3
Interview process, 14, 16, 17, 44, 45
Interview questions, 43
Introverts, 63, 64

K

Knowledge workers, 2, 37

L

Leader, 2–4, 11
    Covid-19, 30
    traditional image, 28
    virtual remote teams, 28
Leadership stereotypes, 29
Leadership style, 27, 29, 37, 39, 41, 102
Learning management system team, 16
Lockdowns, 10

Index

M

Madison College IT, 81
Maslow's hierarchy, 65, 66
Meeting space, 20, 114
Mistake-friendly culture, 61
Monthly all-hands meeting, 47, 50
Motivated remote workforces, 4
Motivated self-starter, 43
Motivation, 69
Motivation-Hygiene theory, 65–67
Motivators, 66
Mullenweg's five-level model, 6

N

Not Another F***ing Tool Syndrome" (NAFTS), 78

O

Office vs. workspace, 25
Onboarding, 54
    digital/paperless, 54
    experiment/iterate, 56
    gear/swag, 55, 56
One-to-one (1:1) meetings, 46
Online teaching, 11
On-site environment, 76, 114
On-site/in-person work, 108
Opportunity, 93–95
Opposing viewpoints
    collaboration
        challenges, 110, 111
    innovation challenges, 110
    onboarding, 109, 110
    protect, 109
    teaching/learning, 111, 112
    Theory X workers, 112, 113
    Theory Y workers, 113
Organizational change, 29, 120
Organizational competency, 34
Organizational
    model, 44, 63, 95
Out-crowd, 76

P

Periodic influxes, 21
Personal connections, 61, 70, 87
Personality types, 58, 63–65
Physical space, 20, 24, 108
Physical workplace, 105
Planning/designing space, 21
Planning process, 19
Preparation phase, 54
Private office, 20, 23
Problem-solving, 49
Productivity
    meetings, 106
    travel, 108
Product team, 7, 9
Project team spaces, 20
Public criticism, 83

Q

Quality assurance (QA), 94

R

Real estate, 12, 18, 19, 109
Recruiting, see Hiring
Reinforcement, 48, 61
Relationship-building, 45
    contact, 46, 47
    empathy, 46
Remote communications, 82
Remote culture-building, 48
    benefits, 49
    leaders, 49
    learning/assessment, 50
    problem-solving, 49
    value accountability, 48
Remote distributed model, 14, 25, 94, 96, 99, 100, 103, 105, 109
Remote distributed organizational models, 8, 12, 116
Remote distributed teams
    leader, 28
    software developers, 33

Remote distributed workforces, 10
Remote distributed work models, 91
Remote distributed workplace, 106
Remote hybrid work, 103, 104, 106
Remote innovation, 104
Remote *vs.* on-site meetings, 106
Remote opposition, 102
Remote relationship, 46
Remote software development teams, 31
Remote virtual technology, 52
Remote workers, 35, 38
Remote work experiment, 119
Remote work model, 2, 15, 19, 37
Remote work options, 32
Remote work policies, 6
Risk mitigation, 10

S

Salesforce, 3, 51, 103, 117
Salesforce automation (SFA), 3
Security team, 17
Self-perpetuating circle, 92
Servant leader, 121
Slack, 3, 52, 54, 79
Social media, 118
Software as a Service (SaaS), 3, 51
Software development teams, 31, 34, 70
Software products, 80
Space utilization models, 21
Standardize repeatable processes, 56
Swift trust, 61, 62
Synchronous communication, 84

T

Teams, 3–6, 76
Technical talent, 17

Technology-oriented people, 56
Telemedicine, 37, 97, 98
Temporary collaboration, 20
Theory X, 68, 112, 121
Theory Y, 68, 69, 113
Three-Letter Acronyms (TLA), 54
Travel, 17
Trust, 59, 60
Trustworthy, 89

U

User acceptance testing (UAT), 99
User interfaces (UI), 3

V

Video conference meetings, 50
Video-conferencing tools, 38
Virtual care, 37
Virtual global organization, 88
Virtual meetings, 119
Virtual reality (VR), 112, 118
Voice Over Internet Protocol (VOIP), 3

W, X, Y

Walking conference call, 36
Whiteboarding apps, 77
WordPress, 15, 16, 48, 80
Workforce, diversity, 17
Work-from-home models, 107
Working styles, 42
Workplace generations, 59
Workplace culture, 51, 105
Workplaces, 119
Work scenario, 30, 51, 63, 65, 67

Z

Zoom, 3, 79

GPSR Compliance

The European Union's (EU) General Product Safety Regulation (GPSR) is a set of rules that requires consumer products to be safe and our obligations to ensure this.

If you have any concerns about our products, you can contact us on

ProductSafety@springernature.com

In case Publisher is established outside the EU, the EU authorized representative is:

Springer Nature Customer Service Center GmbH
Europaplatz 3
69115 Heidelberg, Germany

www.ingramcontent.com/pod-product-compliance
Lightning Source LLC
LaVergne TN
LVHW010343260326
834688LV00036B/850